LEAVE TO CLEAVE
Marriage As A Life Long Commitment

LEAVE TO CLEAVE
Marriage As A Life Long Commitment

OLULEKE AKINOLA

PYXIDIA HOUSE PUBLISHERS

Scripture quotations are from the Holy Bible: New International
Version (NIV), The Message (MSG), New King James Version
(NKJV), King James Version (KJV).

Request for information on this title should be addressed to
Oluleke Akinola
Upper Baptist Church, Lagos, Nigeria
Email: lekeakinola@yahoo.co.uk
+234 803 565 2137

Library of Congress Cataloging-in-Publication Data

Oluleke Akinola
LEAVE TO CLEAVE - *Marriage As A Life Long Commitment*
ISBN-13: 978-1-946530-20-2 (Paperback)
ISBN-10: 1-946530-20-4 (Paperback)
1. Religion - Christianity - Marriage - Non-fiction 1. Title
Library of Congress Control Number: 2019949800

Edited by Winnie Aduayi

Published in Dallas Texas by Pyxidia House Publishers. A registered
trademark of Pyxidia Concept llc. www.pyxidiahouse.com
info@pyxidiahouse.com

Printed in the United States of America

To the wonderful and gracious Almighty God, who in His mercy has led me all the way and blessed my home with a Christian testimony. May His name be glorified.

To all men and women who have, by God's grace, decided to make the best out of their marriage. You will not fail in Jesus name.

To my wife, Oyeboade Oluyemisi Akinola, who has indeed been a support and destiny helper.

Acknowledgements

I give all glory and honour to God, who has helped me in the journey of life and gave me a family that models what has been put down in this book.

I especially thank my wife, Mrs Oyeboade Akinola, who without her help, I will not qualify to write a book on marriage. Together we have raised a godly family that is an example of a Christian home. More so, this book would have been impossible without her encouragements, advice and the fact that she made her expertise available as my first editor.

I appreciate my children, Tomiwa, Dolapo,

Timi, Tinu, Tooni and my grandchild, Oluwatorera; we learnt to raise godly children through our dealings with them.

I thank God for all the couples that have gone through our pre-marital counselling sessions in the last 15 years. We daily improve as we spend time with them. Much of the contents of this book are from our experiences with them, as led by the Holy Spirit.

Mrs Idowu Olaoye and Shade Fapohunda were very helpful in typing the first draft and subsequent updates of the book. You are appreciated. I also appreciate Bro. Gbolahan Osinowo, who secretly took the first draft of this book to the editor, for the first edits and set the pace for the journey.

I appreciate our brother, Pastor Babatunde Ale for helping to proofread the manuscript, spending an entire night working on it. Thanks, bro.

Without Upper Room Baptist Church I may not have a platform to exhibit the grace of God upon my life; I thank all the council members, pastors, and members of the Church for your unflinching support through these years. May His grace see us through, and His work will continue to grow in our hands in Jesus name.

I want to appreciate the Chairman of the Pentecostal Fellowship of Nigeria, Lagos State, Bishop Olusola Ore, who in such short notice wrote the foreword of this book. Thanks, sir.

My heart goes to the Developmental Editor, Winnie Aduayi, for doing a great job to make this book what it is today. She is a professional. Thank God the battle is over and we can laugh at last.

Finally, my appreciation goes to everyone that will read this book, and not just read it, but also apply the wisdom of God in it. To those who are having a good time in their marriage, there is always room for improvement. And to those who are struggling, it is never too late for you to benefit from one of God's great gift to mankind: Marriage. Submit your life and marriage to

God and see Him turn around the situation for the best.

Thank you.

Contents

Foreword

One of the greatest threats to the future of our world is the carnal idealism of marriage. Over the past generation, the world has changed at a meteoric rate. The marriage institution stands at the forefront of this change, and also stands at a critical crossroads, floating in a sea of relativism and broken homes. It seems evident over the past decades we have failed to see the adverse ripple effects of misplaced and misguided ideologies of marriage on society. Against this backdrop, Oluleke Akinola enlightens and challenges married couples and would-be married couples to raise the bar.

Why is the marriage institution that powerful and influential? Because marriage is not a social, cultural, religous, or political construct; instead, it is divine and finds its power in the personal chambers of the soul of the individuals. It is within the soul that the divine melts humanity, and it is where we discover the source of the private motivation that forms our perceptions and behaviour. Hence, the author, Pastor Oluleke Akinola, painstakingly and carefully takes the reader to the origin of marriage and how a Christian marriage should be. He not only wrote from his experience but also succinctly took us through what the responsibilities of each partner in the union should be in the eyes of God.

Marriage, he says, takes maturity and the fear of God to succeed; hence it is not for boys and girls but between men and women.

The book is well laid out in sequential order, which makes reading quite compelling. It is also a great book that can be described as a manual on marriage. It is recommended as a marriage counselling handbook for intending couples, and a reference manual for both young and older couples.

Bishop (Dr.) Sola Ore
Chairman
Pentecostal Fellowship of Nigeria, Lagos State.

Introduction

In the world of architecture and building, understanding and working with a blueprint is necessary before you can successfully implement a design. The same principle applies to the institution of marriage; understanding the blueprint or plan for marriage helps it work at its optimal when we align ourselves with the design. I cannot tell you that marriage is easy to maintain, but neither is anything else that is valuable and worthwhile. The blueprint tells us how things work in this unique institution, which we must endeavour to follow if we must succeed. However, unlike the blueprint for high-performance engineering that is designed by man, this blueprint comes from the loving heart of our Father and Creator, God, who wants His people to have meaningful, peaceful and loving relationships. It's important to remember that marriage is God's idea. Marriage is not just a social construct or an idea that man came up with as a good option for society; no, it is not. Marriage is written into the very fabric of creation as God's normative pattern for the growth and development of humanity, and the roles of husband and wife are both reflections of His extravagant love. Thus, we cannot change the rules or tamper with the design and still expect it to work optimally.

Today, many marriages are a study in chaos. Dysfunction and malice flare as many couples attack each other, and others resort to the cold war, while their children run the gamut of 'all things defiant', looking for answers in all the wrong places. Ultimately, these couples and their children become the victims of broken homes and misdirected lives. Marriage is at the core of the heart of God because He knows that the devil cannot run our nations, our states, our communities or our children unless he first destroys the marital home front.

If there's anything that has experienced the fiercest attack of the devil in recent times, it is the marriage institution. We hear reports of insurgencies in nations, killings happening in schools, and many vices being perpetrated by people, and you wonder where it all started from. It started from the home. When a father could not think of anything else to present his son as a birthday gift but a gun, what does the society expect of that child? What was that man's frame of mind while handing over a weapon of mass destruction to his son? This happened in one of the states in America, where a teenage boy took the gun to school and shot at people indiscriminately, taking the lives of many. This is a society where you can't even throw stones at squirrels. You can't kill any straying rabbit or antelope because even animals have the right to life, yet killing humans appear to be normal for the perpetrators. How did this boy convince himself to kill people just like that? What was going through his mind? This problem can only be traced to a failure in the family system.

We all know that when the foundation of a building is destroyed, that building will only fall and destroy everything in its wake. That is what happens when we alter the design of what is already built and completed: The marriage institution was completed and established at creation by God for us to go into using His blueprint. Hence, if marriage is God's normative pattern for the growth and development of humanity, it then means that marriage is only possible between a male and a female because the growth of the human race is only possible between this two kinds – male and female, not any other design man has created to suit his lustful pleasures. All attempts to change this blueprint only speak further to the failure of the family system.

Many developed countries now celebrate same-sex marriage. It's gotten to an alarming point whereby any church or pastor that refuses to join two gay people is exposed to closure or prosecution. But God did not create Steve to marry Steven neither did He create Mary for Martha. This evil form of marriage which was practised in Sodom and Gomorrah in the book of *Genesis 18* and *19* was the reason God destroyed that city. We may be saying all is well with us today; what about tomorrow?

The countries where same-sex marriages were fought for and eventually legalized may not have seen it coming years back, but because at some point they lost a grip of their moral standards, especially from the family units, it crept upon them. It started creeping into their system unnoticed long before they discovered it. That's how the devil operates; he will come in gradually until he grabs you at a place where you have no choice but to surrender; that place where you either lack knowledge of God's blueprint or decided to alter it to serve your selfish interest. Thus, today, Steve and Steven can go to one Pastor Cornelius or Bishop Zea and would be declared husband and wife in matrimony, and people will celebrate; likewise, Eve and Eva. Yet, you wonder where it all started from. Only a breakdown in the family values of a society that can cause such occurrences.

When you go to under bridges and markets in Lagos, Nigeria, you will find some children roaming about, running errands for some street thugs, whom they consider their 'area father' or godfather. They value and respect him more than their biological parents or guardians if they have any. This brings to mind a story that was shared with us in secondary school: A boy was late to school and was sent back home by the Principal to get his father. However, he didn't go home; instead, he went to 'under the bridge' and called a thug, and the man showed up, claiming to be the father of the boy, not caring that the Principal and other students knew that was not his father. Another story was told of an under-age boy who came to school with his father's expensive briefcase containing a pack of cigarette and was quite defiant about it when the teacher confronted him. These incidents could only happen as a result of a home experiencing a breakdown.

Many do not know what it really entails to be married. Some, probably, got married because their friends were getting married. It's utterly appalling to see some marriages end on the same day it started. A long time ago, a friend of mine got married to the daughter of one of the richest men in Nigeria; on their wedding day they received the most expensive car as a gift from the lady's father. The marriage lasted barely three months. The problem started at the

Reception Hall where they had their wedding, and just like that the marriage was over.

Everyone wants to experience a great marriage that will last. The most effective and fulfilling way to achieve that goal is by consulting the Master Creator, God, who created marriage in the first place. Some of us put the blame of a failing or failed marriage on the other spouse. Some even blame the children for the problems existing between them. Why not look inwards? When you know what is expected of you, the unique role each spouse plays in a marriage, and you are playing your role according to God's plan; taking every situation to Him and reminding Him of His promises concerning marriage, your marriage will be successful.

More than ever before, this book comes in handy at such a time as we live in today. We shall be looking into what marriage really is; the origin of marriage, the reason God instituted marriage, the prerequisite for harmony in a home, role-playing, and the principle of love. It is my prayer that the Lord touches every home going through a hard time now, in Jesus name, amen.

Author's Note

If the word *'community'* is critically examined, you will find that it is made up of the family. That is why we encourage that a man and his wife be part of the same community of believers: Church. It is expected that when a man marries a woman, she moves with him to his Church, but most importantly, they should attend the same Church. Attending separate places of worship is not healthy for marriage; it is invariably separating the home. It is absolutely wrong for any Church to encourage a man and his wife to attend two different Churches for the sake of maintaining their numbers. We must all obey God. I hope that you open your heart to receive this teaching.

Chapter One
The State Of Marriage Today

The Bible draws a clear link between the everlasting covenant between God and His people and the marriage covenant between husband and wife. Our marriages are designed to mirror Christ's marriage to the Church in both purpose and permanence. However, most people, rather than strive to discover and embrace ultimate truths about marriage, are captivated by the world's ideals of marriage, even though events around us make it painfully clear that when it comes to marriage, the world has got it all wrong.

Marriage is no longer what it used to be. It is no longer aligning to God's original intentions, with much controversies around it. Sometime in the early 2000s, US Talk Show host, Bill O'Reilly told viewers that of all the controversial things he wrote in his book, *'The O'Reilly Factor'*, he got the worst backlash over the chapter on marriage about his statement that *"marriage is vitally important to having a good life."* O'Reilly and his guest on the show that day both agreed that marriage had become a most controversial issue, as marriage critics continue the backlash, while claiming that all lifestyles are good, depending on individual choice, there is no one way of living that is more important than the other, and that marriage is just another lifestyle.

Something is fundamentally wrong with the culture! Marriage is not a lifestyle nor a mere human invention. Marriage is a sacred institution. If marriage was no more than a lifestyle or social construct that man came up with, then, no doubt, the different types of marriage in the world today would have equal value, but that is not the case. Marriage is God's creation, and that means that only God defines what it is. As a matter of fact, man has no right to decide the type of marital relationships that should exist, although that hasn't stopped people from trying.

Studying the book of Genesis, you will find that Adam did not institute marriage. God did. Adam didn't just wake up to a need for a wife; he felt no such need, the thought never even occurred to him, if he felt the need for one, he could have chosen any of the animals and married one seeing there was no other human but him existing. God is the Master Creator, who is in the business of perfection of all things; it was solely His idea to perfect His created world and grow humanity through the union between a man and a woman. Thus, He observed and said that it was not good for man to be alone, so He made him a woman. God chose a woman for the man because two men or two women cannot produce children. Anything outside of this should not be called marriage in the first place. Marriage is divine. Marriage is good. So, if we must get married, we must do it as unto God. If marriage is not well handled, a person may end up in hell for not obeying the precepts of God in it. Marriage is sacred and should not be toyed with.

Gay and lesbian marriages are wrong! And it gets even worse: Now, if you have a dog or a cat that you love so much, you can take that animal to the marriage registry and be legally married to it in some countries. Thus, an official is obligated to join Mr. John and his dog, Bingo, and declare them man and wife, or should I say, 'man and animal'. You can imagine! This is a clear case of the world suffering from pervasive lack of reverence for moral values and godliness. We mock the sacred and worship the secular. Depravity is on the increase. Unholy sexual practices are now commonplace between husband and wife. People even engage in trial or sample marriages; a form of contract marriage where an agreement is reached between the couple involved to be married for a certain period to test their compatibility. If they feel compatible enough, they continue the marriage, but if not, the marriage will be dissolved. This form of marriage can be likened to going to the market to buy *Garri*, and you would first take a small sample to taste at home to know whether it is sweet enough for you to purchase or not. Strangely enough, you hear some divorcée tell you that they annulled their marriage because they are not sexually compatible. What does that tell you? Compatibility, in this sense, should have to do more with cars, not marriage. All these were not the plan of God for marriage from the beginning.

Today, we have all kinds of broken homes: Families who may be living together, with children, and both parents are sharing the same bed, but the bed is compartmentalized with pillows in between them. And the children too don't see eye to eye with one another. This kind of situation occurred in the Bible in the family of Isaac.

Isaac was a prosperous man, but he failed in his family life. Isaac took Esau as his favourite son while Rebecca, his wife, took Jacob as her favourite. The two sons were at rivalry because of their parents' choice of family life. Father and mother were playing the deadly game of favouritism; choosing sides and competing to outdo one another with their children. The drama didn't start in one day, as some may think. Esau was a hunter and knew how to please his father. He would catch a game and prepare it to his father's delight. I am sure Jacob must have tried a few tricks to have a taste of Esau's meal on a few occasions, but Isaac never instilled harmony in his home, and it eventually tore his family apart. It was a dysfunctional family; his sons turned against each other.

Unfortunately, many haven't learnt a thing from Isaac's experience, so the same scenarios are still playing out in many families today. A parent wants all the children to love him or her alone, and so often comes home with gifts to impress them so that in his or her old age they would take care of him or her more than the other parent, not because the parent loves their children; it's all about manipulating them to serve his or her selfish purpose. However, as parents, both of you are supposed to love each other first; when you do so, love automatically flows to your children, and you will see unity among the children. Have you not heard of cases when children born of the same parents fight each other with *juju* (voodoo) just to gain the love of their parents? Such a family is a broken family. This is not the plan of God for marriage. In some terrible cases, some women are severely abused by their husbands, and some women also abuse their husbands. I have seen a woman beat her husband on a few occasions when he provoked her, and she would sit on him on the floor while he pleaded for mercy.

Abuse is not only when you physically assault your spouse. It could be psychological or emotional. For instance, you live with a wife who is never happy because of some things you do, like preferring the fellowship and company of your friends than hers. More often than not, when you leave the office, you will go somewhere to hang out with friends, and because you claim to be born again you will not take alcohol or smoke with them, so you buy a pack of juice for yourself and enjoy their company. You drink your juice, and they drink their beer, while this woman that loves you so much would stay up expecting you at home. Midnight you are not yet back. Do you know what you are doing? You are abusing your wife emotionally. You are destroying your life and your family.

When a woman has to beg you every time to

buy her clothes that her mates are buying, and you continually refuse, not that you don't have the money, but because you want to punish her with money; you are abusing your wife. You deprive of her of sex because you know that she is faithful and committed to only you, and you make excuses. She is an abused woman.

You maltreat your husband when you sit down with your children to discuss negative things about him and make him lose respect before them. When he calls his son, he becomes reluctant to respond to his father because you have poisoned his heart towards his father. He is not getting the best from either his children or from you, his wife; he is an abused man. These are the kind of homes that we have today.

Also, neglected and abused children are not farfetched in some families. How are they neglected or abused? In so many different ways! One of which is, you have money but to pay their school fees is a problem for you. They would be disgraced out of school, and you would, more than likely, incur their wrath eventually, and you, the abuser, ultimately becomes the abused; thus, the cycle of abuse continues.

An incident happened once with one of my children. He got admitted into a secondary school, and it was his first day at school. So, the principal came up with a threat that the school would go through their records to fish out and disgrace anyone who had gained admission into the school through illegal means. My son got back and said, *"Daddy, I hope my admission is not illegal because a threat has been issued, and I don't want to be disgraced."* I laughed over it and reassured him that his admission was genuine. This experience with my son showed me firsthand how traumatised a child can be just by the thought of being disgraced, let alone experience disgrace publicly.

Some of us don't know what we do to our children. You have money, and you are supposed to pay school fees; not that you cannot afford it, but you are just negligent. So, when the roll call for the debtors is announced, your child will be among them. It is shameful and humiliating for that child, but even worse, psychologically damaging. If you don't have the money, it's understandable. Even so, there is a way you can approach the school authority so that your child doesn't get embarrassed. I have done that before! I pleaded with the Principal to save my child the shame of being sent out of school when things were tough for me. I promised to pay at a later date, which I did! The children you abuse, you ignorantly send to places they are not supposed to go.

Sinful relationships abound; you are married, but you know what you do outside your marriage. Your friends encourage you that it is normal to have an extramarital affair. They plant evil seeds in your heart to make you question the trust you have for your spouse. They would ask you whether you know what goes on with your spouse when you are not with them. Any man without a mistress is not a real man anymore. The world is so perverted that such evil has become normal.

As Christians, we ought to be different; God wants to boast about us. We have been bought with a price. Old things have passed away!

Behold everything has become new. So, your family has to be new too. God wants to use each of our families as an example of a good family. See how God boasted about Job and Abraham. He said He Knew Abraham as a man who would command his household in the way of the Lord. He could not keep his secret from Abraham because he trusted Abraham to teach his children and grandchildren to fear the Lord. He was a godly role model for his family.

Gen.18: 17-19 records God's thoughts about Abraham:

> Then GOD said, "Shall I keep back from Abraham what I'm about to do? Abraham is going to become a large and strong nation; all the nations of the world are going to find themselves blessed through him. Yes, I've settled on him as the one to train his children and future family to observe GOD's way of life, live kindly and generously and fairly, so that GOD can complete in Abraham what he promised him." (MSG).

God wants to build something special with us.

Many of us are losing the blessings that God has prepared for us because we are not building our homes. Many would say, "do as I say, don't do as I do," which is not supposed to be so. God trusted Abraham to teach his household to do righteousness and justice, so He fulfilled that which he had promised him.

God has a plan for your life. As at the time God chose me, I didn't know what God had in mind for me neither did I understand my purpose. But He gave me a wife that is perfect for me. One who is super comparable, adaptable, complementary and just right for me because He knew where I was going.

That is why when people come to me with their marriage options, especially those whom I know God has a specific purpose for, I tell them to go and pray so that they can hear from God. Because it is only your God-given spouse that has the grace to not only complement you perfectly but also help you fulfil purpose. When God calls a man, he carefully selects his wife for him because of his purpose. But if you marry just anyone, you may end up settling for a counterfeit, and then you begin to blame God.

Let's look again at The Message Bible translation of **Gen. 18:19**:

> *"Yes, I've settled on him as the one to train his children and future family to observe GOD's way of life, live kindly and generously and fairly, so that GOD can complete in Abraham what he promised him."* (MSG)

God desires to give you a family that people can reference as the family of God; a family worth emulating. There was a standing promise in the life of Abraham that was to be fulfilled if he commanded his household to fear the Lord and walk before Him. Thus, being the seed of Abraham, as children of God, there is a standing promise upon our lives which must be fulfilled. The promises God made to Abraham were not just about Abraham alone but also for you and me. That is the reason why we cannot treat our family with levity, live our lives anyhow or marry just anyone.

Sometimes, when certain young people present their marriage options to us, we discourage them from going further into marriage with such spouses after we must have sought God's face and found that God did not support their choices. Some would heed our advice to avoid a dangerous marriage while some would not. You cannot force your members not to marry whom they want to marry; they will go and get married in another church. Ours is to guide them from making marital mistakes by speaking the truth because we know the consequences of marrying wrongly. Don't get me wrong, this is not to say that when you marry the right person, you will not have problems. No; it will require real effort from both of you to make a godly marriage. A good marriage, just like anything worthwhile, takes commitment and doing the right things every day.

When God created you, He made provision for you as to whom you would marry. The person may be around you, and you might not identify the person. As you keep waiting on God, He sure will reveal that person to you. You may not have money or fame, but even the richest person on earth may not be as happy as you are because when you obey God and connect to your God-given spouse, you both would live a happy and fulfilled life. Let's examine a story in the Bible of two families; first one is in **1 Sam. 25: 1-38**:

"Samuel died. The whole country came to his funeral. Everyone grieved over his death, and he was buried in his hometown of Ramah. Meanwhile, David moved again, this time to the wilderness of Maon.

There was a certain man in Maon who carried on his business in the region of Carmel. He was very prosperous — three thousand sheep and a thousand goats, and it was sheep-shearing time in Carmel. The man's name was Nabal (Fool), a Calebite, and his wife's name was Abigail. The woman was intelligent and good-looking, the man brutish and mean.

David, out in the backcountry, heard that Nabal was shearing his sheep and sent ten of his young men off with these instructions: "Go to Carmel and approach Nabal. Greet him in my name, 'Peace! Life and peace to you. Peace to your household, peace to everyone here! I heard that it's sheep-shearing time. Here's the point: When your shepherds were camped near us we didn't take advantage of them. They didn't lose a thing all the time they were with us in Carmel. Ask your young men—they'll tell you. What I'm asking is that you be generous with my men—share the feast! Give whatever your heart tells you to your servants and to me, David your son."

David's young men went and delivered his message word for word to Nabal. Nabal tore into them, "Who is this David? Who is this son of Jesse? The country is full of runaway servants these days. Do you think I'm going to take good bread and wine and meat freshly butchered for my sheepshearers and give it to men I've never laid eyes on? Who knows where they've come from?"

David's men got out of there and went back and told David what he had said. David said, "Strap on your swords!" They all strapped on their swords, David and his men, and set out, four hundred of them. Two hundred stayed behind to guard the camp. Meanwhile, one of the young shepherds told Abigail, Nabal's wife, what had happened: "David sent messengers from the backcountry to salute our master, but he tore into them with insults. Yet these men treated us very well. They took nothing from us and didn't take advantage of us all the time we were in the fields. They formed a wall around us, protecting us day and night all the time we were out tending the sheep. Do something quickly because big trouble is ahead for our master and all of us. Nobody can talk to him. He's impossible—a real brute!"

Abigail flew into action. She took two hundred loaves of bread, two skins of wine, five sheep dressed out and ready for cooking, a bushel of roasted grain, a hundred raisin cakes, and two hundred fig cakes, and she had it all loaded on some donkeys. Then she said to her young servants, "Go ahead and pave the way for me. I'm right behind you."

But she said nothing to her husband Nabal. As she was riding her donkey, descending into a ravine, David and his men were descending from the other end, so they met there on the road. David had just said, "That sure was a waste, guarding everything this man had out in the wild so that nothing he had was lost—and now *he rewards me with insults. A real slap in the face! May God do his worst to me if Nabal and every cur in his misbegotten brood aren't dead meat by morning!"*

As soon as Abigail saw David, she got off her donkey and fell on her knees at his feet, her face to the ground in homage, saying, "My master, let me take the blame! Let me speak to you. Listen to what I have to say. Don't dwell on what that brute Nabal did. He acts out the meaning of his name: Nabal, Fool. Foolishness oozes from him.

"I wasn't there when the young men my master sent arrived. I didn't see them. And now, my master, as GOD lives and as you live, GOD has kept you from this avenging murder — and may your enemies, all who seek my master's harm, end up like Nabal! Now take this gift that I, your servant girl, have brought to my master, and give it to the young men who follow in the steps of my master.

"Forgive my presumption! But GOD is at work in my master, developing a rule solid and dependable. My master fights GOD's battles! As long as you live

no evil will stick to you.

If anyone stands in your way, if anyone tries to get you out of the way, Know this: Your God-honored life is tightly bound in the bundle of God-protected life; But the lives of your enemies will be hurled aside as a stone is thrown from a sling.

"When GOD completes all the goodness he has promised my master and sets you up as prince over Israel, my master will not have this dead weight in his heart, the guilt of an avenging murder. And when GOD has worked things for good for my master, remember me."

And David said, "Blessed be GOD, the God of Israel. He sent you to meet me! And blessed be your good sense! Bless you for keeping me from murder and taking charge of looking out for me. A close call! As GOD lives, the God of Israel who kept me from hurting you, if you had not come as quickly as you did, stopping me in my tracks, by morning there would have been nothing left of Nabal but dead meat."

Then David accepted the gift she brought him and said, "Return home in peace. I've heard what you've said and I'll do what you've asked."

When Abigail got home she found Nabal presiding over a huge banquet. He was in high spirits—and very, very drunk. So she didn't tell him anything of what she'd done until morning. But in the morning, after Nabal had sobered up, she told him the whole story. Right then and there he had a heart attack and fell into a coma. About ten days later GOD finished him off and he died.

It is the story of Abigail and Nabal, her husband, and that of David. David had saved and protected the flocks of Nabal when they were in danger with marauders and a time came for Nabal to return the favours when David and his men needed food. So, David sent his men to approach Nabal since they had once helped him, but instead of helping, this man insulted them, humiliated them and sent them away empty-handed. David vowed to avenge himself and kill Nabal but was stopped by the wise and virtuous wife of Nabal; she saved her husband from David's wrath and also delivered David from the sin of avenging himself, which God has said it is for him alone to handle. That's why you must marry rightly. It would be best if you learned to overlook the physical appearance of a person because those things will always definitely change.

I was praying for a 36-year-old lady some years back who was seeking God's face for a husband. While we prayed, the Lord asked me to stop and ask her why she wasn't married yet, which I did. Apparently, she has been very selective of the men that approached her; they didn't meet the standard she had set for herself. I asked her to cry to God for mercy because she had missed her husband several years back.

When my wife decided to marry me, I was not marriageable by worldly standard. I had only two pairs of jeans trousers, one pair of shoes, which was a canvas, three T-shirts and two pairs of football boots. So anywhere we went I always wore that one pair of canvas. I remember the first time she invited me for an occasion; I didn't know what to wear, so I had to involve a friend who took me out to shop for some good clothes in the market. When my wife saw me, she was very happy and surprised at how I was able to achieve that because she was already becoming worried for me. I was not qualified for marriage material-wise, but she invested well. If you look at a person's present state and use that to judge their future, you may end up missing it. Verses 18 and 19 of the above scripture says:

> *Abigail flew into action. She took two hundred loaves of bread, two skins of wine, five sheep dressed out and ready for cooking, a bushel of roasted grain, a hundred raisin cakes, and two hundred fig cakes, and she had it all loaded on some donkeys. Then she said to her young servants, "Go ahead and pave the way for me. I'm right behind you." But she said nothing to her husband Nabal.*

Abigail was a wise woman. Maybe if she had told Nabal of her intentions, he would have threatened her as most men would. Maybe he would have said, *"if you go and meet David, better don't come back to this house again. You better just marry him from there because am going to disown you and your children."* That would have been prophetic on his side.

What is the conclusion of this matter? It was this woman that saved David from committing murder because he could have destroyed the entire household of Nabal, including Abigail.

The next family I would talk about is found in the book of Acts; Ananias and Sapphira. It is a very fantastic story with many lessons to draw from it. The quality of your marriage choice would surely determine the quality of your life and how long you would live.

In **Acts 5**, the disciples were being multiplied and with it came an increase in their basic needs. So, people sold some of their possessions and brought the proceeds to the Apostles to cater to everyone's need. Barnabas was one man who sold his possession and gave all the proceeds generously to the Church. This action earned him a title among the early Church as the son of consolation. This must have brought about envy in the heart of Ananias and Sapphira that they too decided to sell their own possession so that they also would donate and be recognized by the Church.

They sold their piece of possession, but both

of them agreed in one accord to lie to the Church about the percentage of their proceeds. The Holy Spirit killed them instantly because they conspired to deceive their leaders and the Holy Spirit.

Sapphira could have saved her family if she refused to collude with her husband to deceive the Church. A woman is supposed to help her husband to succeed, but she helped her husband and supported him in his evil plan, and they both paid for it with their lives.

While Abigail saved her home with her wisdom, Sapphira destroyed hers with her foolishness. **Prov. 12:4** couldn't be more apt when it says, *"A virtuous woman is a crown to her husband."* A woman honours God by becoming a real help meet to her husband.

Chapter Two
The Purpose Of God For Marriage

There has never been a generation in the world whose general view of marriage is high enough. The disparity between God's vision of marriage and the human view has always been wide. No doubt, some cultures respect the importance and permanence of marriage; still, many more have such low, casual attitude towards marriage much that it makes the biblical vision appear ridiculous to most people.

Back in the old days, in **Matt. 19:4-9**, when Jesus gave a glimpse of the magnificent view of marriage that God planned for His children, the disciples said to Him in **Matt. 19:10**,

"If such is the case of a man with his wife, it is better not to marry." In other words, God's vision of marriage was so remarkably different from the disciples understanding of the institution, so much that they couldn't even imagine it to be a good thing. If the disciples thought this way in a time when the world was sober, how much more will the magnificence of marriage as God purposed appear unfathomable in today's modern culture, where self-centeredness and disobedience reign supreme, with the overbearing influences of the media and the internet, and the demand of their altar is the uninhibited sexual indiscretion.

So, the question is, why did God institute marriage? What is God's purpose for man?

Firstly, the most foundational truth we must understand in consideration of the purpose of marriage is that marriage is from God and through God; there is no other source. Then, the ultimate truth about marriage is that it is not only from God and through God; marriage is for God. Marriage exists for God's glory; it is designed by God to display His glory in a way that no other institution does; thus, it cannot be treated nonchalantly.

Reading **Gen. 2:24** and connecting it with **Eph. 5:31 – 32**, makes it clearer. In **Gen. 2:24**, God says, *"Therefore a man shall leave his father and mother and hold fast to his wife and they shall become one flesh."* These words *"hold fast to his wife"* and *"they shall become one flesh"*, point to a union that is designed to be much deeper and more permanent than we know it to be. An easy illustration would be to glue two sheets of paper together. Now, when you try to separate the papers after pasting together, you would end up completely destroying both papers because the potency of the glue wouldn't let them come apart as it was before you stuck them together. Thus, these words imply one truth, which is that marriage is a sacred relationship rooted in a covenant commitment that must not be broken even in the face of adversity. It gets even broader when Paul further spoke about marriage quoting **Gen. 2:24** in **Eph. 5:31-32**, *"Therefore a man shall leave his father and mother and hold fast to his wife and they shall become one flesh,"* and then sums it up in **verse 32** by saying, *"This mystery is profound, and I am saying that it refers to Christ and the Church."* Simply put, marriage is modelled after Christ's covenant commitment to the Church.

Therefore, the ultimate purpose of marriage is for our marriages - "husband and wife", to showcase to the world the glorious nature and depth of the covenant relationship between Christ and His Church (*We will discuss this in more detail later in this chapter*). Your marriage is a physical model of Christ and the Church, His bride, whom He paid for with His blood. That is why marriage exists; why you are married – to show the world the glorious love and unbreakable bond that Christ has for His Church. For this reason, your obedience to God's Word means everything in your marriage. Marriage is from God, through God, and for God; thus, the beauty and joy of marriage can only be fully appreciated and enjoyed by obeying His Word.

When the Word of God is taught by the power of the Holy Spirit, it is our obedience to the Word that activates the power of that Word in our lives. For instance, if the Word of God says that a wife should submit to your own husband, and the woman begins to rationalize why she shouldn't, then what God wants to achieve with your submission will definitely not be achieved because you are resisting God. Similarly, if God says a man should love his wife as Christ loves the Church and the man says, "thank God, I'm not Jesus!" That goes to show how much he wants to rule his family without God.

The way these things work is for us to believe the Word of God and obey. Even when what you are seeing is not looking like what it is supposed to be, but because God has said it, we obey.

God designed marriage in such a way that it does not work as effectively as it should without Him. Let's look at an illustration based on **Eccl. 4:12** which says, *"A person standing alone can be attacked and defeated, but two can stand back-to-back and conquer. Three are even better, for a triple-braided cord is not easily broken."* (NLT). The three represent God, husband, and wife.

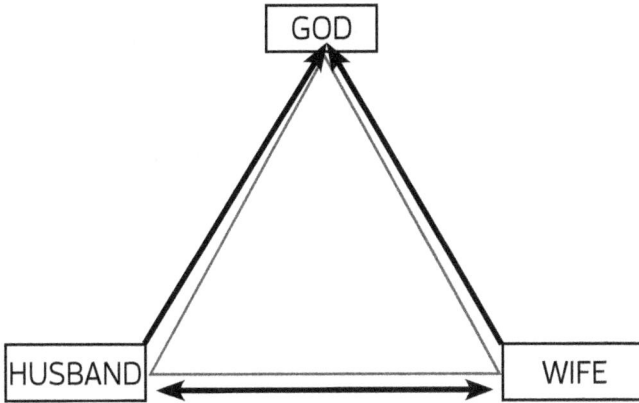

Now, place a finger from your left and right hand on each point that says 'husband' and 'wife' (your fingers represent each spouse), then slowly move your fingers up the two sides to the point that says, 'God'. When you get to that point, you will find that your fingers are close together and touching. The point here is quite profound: the closer you both grow to God, the closer you and your spouse would grow to each other, and you cannot be broken apart, because God is like the glue holding you together, so none can successfully tear you apart without going through God first. Notice that when you are both not moving towards God, you remain apart at the bottom. The greatest thing you can do for your marriage is to live as one with

God; to live as one with God is to obey and live His Word.

Furthermore, notice that **Eccl. 4:12** used the term *"not easily broken"* rather than "can never be broken". Why is that? Because God is unchanging and ever guaranteed not to leave His own, but man always waivers and cannot be guaranteed to stand by God, especially when it gets tough. So, the uncertainty of man influenced the writer of Ecclesiastics to use the term *"not easily broken."* But as long as the couple do not separate themselves from God, then the cord will 'never' be broken, and the marriage will be at its optimal, even in the face of storms.

So, what is going on in your home currently? Are you doing what God expects of you and growing closer to Him? Are you playing your part? If you are, then leave the rest to God, the result is God's! However, disobedience to what God expects of His children has led many of us to ignorantly let the devil take over our homes. You shift the blame to your spouse, and your spouse does the same, without considering looking inwards to ask yourself truthful questions like: What am I doing wrong in this family? What am I doing, inaccurately? You know, you may not be wrong, but still not be doing the right thing at the right time. Until you are ready to obey God, the teachings you've heard will not be productive in your life.

Gen. 2:18-22:

And the LORD God said, It is not good that the man should be alone; I will make him an help meet for him.

And out of the ground the LORD God formed every beast of the field, and every fowl of the air; and brought them unto Adam to see what he would call them: and whatsoever Adam called every living creature, that was the name thereof.

And Adam gave names to all cattle, and to the fowl of the air, and to every beast of the field; but for Adam there was not found an help meet for him.

And the LORD God caused a deep sleep to fall upon Adam, and he slept: and he took one of his ribs, and closed up the flesh instead thereof;

And the rib, which the LORD God had

taken from man, made he a woman, and brought her unto the man. (KJV).

Now, let's delve into more detail on the purpose of God for bringing the man and the woman together. As we already know, it is not mainly for procreation purpose, like some tend to believe. Below are four salient reasons that made God introduce the marriage institution to man:

1) To mirror Christ's marriage to the Church. This is the first and most important, as we have earlier established.

2) Companionship. This has been regarded as the primary reason for marriage for a long time.

3) Sexual Satisfaction without sin.

4) Procreation. Childbearing.

TO MIRROR CHRIST'S MARRIAGE TO THE CHURCH
Eph: 5:22-25:
"Submitting yourselves one to another in

the fear of God. Wives, submit yourselves unto your own husbands, as unto the Lord. For the husband is the head of the wife, even as Christ is the head of the church: and he is the saviour of the body. Therefore, as the church is subject unto Christ, so let the wives be to their own husbands in everything. Husbands, love your wives, even as Christ also loved the church, and gave himself for it;" (KJV).

Wives submit to your own husband just as the Church submits to Christ. The husband being in a position of authority in the home does not mean that you, as the wife, is inferior to him; it only means that you are there to help him do his work better, to accomplish purpose as a help meet for him. There is no loss of dignity in submission when it serves a higher purpose. Jesus willingly became a helper to the Father, and the Holy Spirit became a helper to the Son. It takes submission to help someone effectively. Society can only maintain sanity and peaceful co-existence because it is structured so that people must submit to authorities like government, employers, the courts, police, etc. Outside of submission to authority, there would be absolute chaos in any society.

God made you a help meet for your husband so that you can bolster him, making him more productive and efficient at whatever he does. A perfect help meet is one who does not require to be pushed, argued with, and cajoled to submit to her husband. Her readiness to please motivates her to look around and see the things that she knows her husband would like to see done. Such a blessed husband with such a help meet would receive honour from other men as they admire and praise his godly wife, and even more, the world would stand in awe of God, as their marriage showcases His glory.

A wife's submission to her husband, and a husband loving his wife are borne out of genuine love for God. If everything we come to do in Church is not borne out of genuine love for God or has its roots in Christ, then we would be wasting our time. The key factor that differentiates the gathering of the Church from gatherings in clubs and parties is the presence of Jesus Christ as the head of the Church.

There is no controversy as to the order of marriage. God's original plan is still the same today as it was in the beginning; for there to exist an order in the house, as **1Cor. 11:8-9** affirms, *"For the man is not of the woman; but the woman of the man. Neither was the man created for the woman; but the woman for the man."* There is no confusion about this and should not be negotiable. The Bible also confirms the husband is head of the home, and thus, asks the wife to submit to his authority as the Church must submit to Christ. Your family is a small Church. Therefore, as a man, everything you do in that family must bring glory to God as you are a representative of God in that family – the head.

Furthermore, marriage will not work unless the husband learns how to love his wife, not as the world defines love, but as God defines it – without conditions and giving his all for her. As a husband, that means you are given a seemingly tough job of loving your wife as sacrificially as Jesus loves His Church, such that you could actually take a bullet in her place; this may sometimes mean sacrificing your ego and good standing among friends in order to protect your wife. You are required to nourish her, cherish her, and be sensitive to her needs: this is how the wife is designed to receive love. As a husband, you have to create an environment in which your wife will flourish in order to be strong enough to be your helper; if you abuse and break her, she will be too weak to help you. So also, wife, if you abuse and violate him, he will be too damaged to love; Christ-like love requires strength.

Husbands, you must endeavour to always take your position in the home, so that the other parts of the home can function correctly. When you relinquish your role at the family altar to your wife and children, not participating in family devotions, you hand over the spiritual authority of the family to them; this keeps the marriage standing on one leg – your leg is missing. Your marriage is meant to mirror the Jesus-Church relationship to the world. **Verse 24** says:

"Therefore as the Church is subject unto Christ, so let the wives be to their own husbands in everything."

Wives, no matter who your husband is, the Bible says you are to submit to him in all things. God wants to see the Jesus-Church relationship in our homes! Husband love your wife. **Verse 25** says:

> *"Husbands, love your wives, even as Christ also loved the church, and gave himself for it;"*

Let your heart be open to receive this teaching. Do not conclude that this kind of family relationship is not possible in our time. No doubt, to submit to your husband and to love your wife as Christ does the Church are both tough requests, but not impossible; we cannot successfully do it on our own without divine help. That is why God must be involved in our marriages. Jesus is the same yesterday, today and forever. The moment you begin to bring modernity to the Word of God, you set your home up for destruction. The reason why the world is where it is today is that men have rationalized the Word of God. Men now promote gay marriages, and some will even quote Scriptures to back up these abominable claims. Husband love your wife as Christ loved the Church and gave Himself for her. You may make excuses about how terrible she is, but Christ loved the Church while we were yet unlovable and gave Himself for her. You are to love her unconditionally. When there was nothing in us that would make anyone love us, Christ did love us to the point of death on the Cross. If you have this in mind, you would learn to love your wife no matter what. Your home should be able to mirror the sacrificial love of Christ, thereby attracting other people to Christ. The people in your neighbourhood should be able to see Christ through your marriage.

Everyone around you knows what is expected of a Christian that is why when you do anything wrong, they are quick to remind you of your Christian claims. But if you practice other religions and you do something wrong, the world will judge you to be normal. Have you not come across people who have vowed never to attend certain Churches because of the character of their Christian neighbours? They've seen the way they behave in their family, the way they treat each other and their children, and thus, came to that conclusion.

Many of us don't understand that we are giving a bad name to Christ by the way we run our families; people are watching us, and they know the expectation of God from us. When you do not live up to them, it's like throwing stones against your Father's house. We are the epistle the world is reading.

COMPANIONSHIP

"And the LORD God said, It is not good that the man should be alone; I will make him an help meet for him."

When God was giving you a help meet, He did not give you for just no reason but that she may help you fulfill your purpose and that both of you should mirror Christ in the society so that His name may be glorified. He brought the two of you together so that people can look at you and say these, indeed, are Christians. The two of you must stay together. God hates loneliness. He said it is not good. A person can be in a crowd and still be a hundred percent lonely. God discovered this and brought the man and the woman together. It is expected of the man and woman to be in fellowship with each other and have one mind after some time. They will have one mind and also mind the same things. **Phil. 2** talks about this. When a couple has one mind and minds the same things, they would always want to be together.

Some time ago, when Nigerian youths were sent to study abroad on scholarship, some of the men wrote letters to their parents to send them a wife. Usually, a photograph would be sent in response, and if the man liked what he saw, the woman would be married off on his behalf and later sent to meet him. When these two people who have never known each other, live for a few years together, they create a strong bond. The bond would be so strong that people tend to believe that they look alike, having the same facial resemblance. This is quite common with husbands and wives. The expectation of God for them is to live together and bond physically, emotionally, and spiritually.

What do we have in our marriages today?

Separation! You see a couple living under one roof but sleeping in different rooms. Some may sleep in the same room and on the same bed but build a wall of separation with pillows between them and their spouse; they sleep on a compartmentalized bed. This is contrary to the plan of God. Some men or women will tell you that they cannot sleep on the same bed with their wives or husbands because she or he snores. How are you sure that it is not for the fact that you can help her or him out of that snoring habit that God brought you together? If you marry a woman and she suddenly begin to bed wet in your house, what will you then do? That could be one of the reasons God brought the two of you together. When you come to terms with it, you would find a solution. You would learn to set the alarm for every two to three hours through the night to help her or him wake up to ease herself or himself. It may sound absurd, but that is the expectation of God. You are supposed to support each other to fulfill God's purpose.

For companionship to grow, the two of you must always love to be together. In some families, the couple eats separately. The woman will be in the kitchen eating while the man is at the dining table eating. These are not things that will encourage bonding; you must love to do things together. If you take a census of couples who take themselves out on a date after their marriage, you would be amazed at the result. Only a few! These are the things that create bonding. With very little money, you can take your spouse out on a date. Maybe you're able to afford only a bottle of Coke and one Meat Pie; there is love in sharing. Share it between each other and enjoy yourselves. As you do, you strike a conversation, and because the atmosphere is friendly, you will find that there are some things that you may not have been able to tell each other, even on the bed, but you can do so there.

If he loves football go and sit with him and watch it together. As you ask seemingly silly questions about the match, his response and the little body contacts that may occur at that space of time would help you bond. What will it cost you to sit with him to watch that match?

If a married Christian man still goes to Beer parlour or viewing centre to watch a football match, even when he has a television in the house, then there is a problem. If you must go, go with your wife.

There are many things militating against companionship, but if you do not get companionship right, your marriage would be unstable because if you two do not come together often enough, there cannot be a healthy dose of sex. It is companionship that will lead to sexual satisfaction, which then leads to procreation. Get companionship right and every other thing will be settled in your home. You must get it right. Once you have missed this, you have missed everything.
How can one miss companionship?

1. **Unnecessary Attachment To Work:**
One of the things that hinder fellowship and companionship is unnecessary attachment to work; the desire to get rich and acquire the material things of life has driven the family apart. The husband leaves the house very early in the morning and comes back late, and the wife also goes on her way; they spend little

or no time together but keep pursuing their different ambition and career. There is hardly any time to spend together; eventually they begin to drift apart until there is a total breakdown of harmony in the home. This affects the original plan of God for the family.

2. Third-Party Involvements:

The Bible in Gen. 2 tells us that the man will leave his father and mother and cleave to his wife. If anything happens in your family and you go to discuss it with your parents, you are still a boy; you are not yet ripe for marriage. These are the things that batter and destroy companionship in a home. The interventions of parents, friend, or even children in the affairs of a couple are classified as third-party involvements. Many homes would have been wonderful but for the intervention of parents, friends, and even the children. Do you know that it is what you build now with your spouse that will determine how you will live your old age? Your children will soon grow up and leave the house, even if they stay till they are thirty-five years, they would surely go someday. If you build a strong bond or relationship with your children and neglect the bond that is supposed to exist between you and your wife, eventually when your children leave the house for good, you will be left alone with your wife; both of you will become total strangers under one roof. If you stop discussing, eating and doing things with your spouse and divert that attention to your children, you will pay for it in your old age. Many people who have gone through this path can testify to this. This is one major source of loneliness for married couples; when the children have gone to face their different lives, they become lonely or depressed. That is why you see many old people who are mentally unstable because they are lonely, no companion. They behave either like children or downright crazy.

When a prisoner misbehaves in the process of serving his jail term, one of the punishments he is given is to be locked up in solitary confinement. Sometimes they keep the prisoner in question in that solitary confinement for months, but when he is brought out, he is never the same; most times, they come out crazy. God who said it is not good for man to be alone knows that if a man remains alone, he could go insane. So, everything that you need to bond and not ever experience loneliness God has already provided so that when someone asks you a question about your wife in her absence, the answer you would give them will be the exact answers she would give when called up on the phone. Both of you should bond so strong that you can think alike and reason alike.

When your children know that there is a division between the two of you, they will play on your intelligence. They will take advantage of that to make unnecessary demands. But when they know that whatever they tell you your spouse will know; they will think well before coming to you. Also, if your parents or family cannot discuss anything with you in front of your wife, let them forget about it. Your wife must know when you are sending money to your family members because both of you are now one flesh. Same goes for the wife's dealings with her family. You are one in everything.

3. Sex: To Satisfy Sexual Need:
One of the best things God created between a

husband and his wife is sex. Sex is good. Sex is wonderful. God designed sex, not only to fulfill the *"be fruitful and multiply"* command in **Gen. 1:28** but also for our enjoyment because God wants married couples to be passionate lovers. God designed husband and wife to bond in the sexual experience, not only physically but also emotionally and spiritually. According to medical experts, the brain secretes the hormone oxytocin during and after sex, which causes couples, especially men, to want to open up and share what's going on inside. The physical chemistry enhances the connection at every other level. God intentionally wired that bonding in His creation and His design for marriage as a physical means to achieve emotional and spiritual oneness; this makes sex in marriage holy. It is the physical expression of a deeper union that serves its full purpose only in the context of love and covenant commitment of marriage.

Sex is one of the things that God created, which remains a mystery to us all. However, sex outside of marriage is a sin. That is why the Bible encourages those who cannot control their sexual urges to get married on time instead of burning. This is so because God has created man in a way that once a person gets to a particular age, he or she begins to have sexual urges or desires by default. It is the reason why you see a difference in the body make up of a boy when he is becoming a man. His body becomes firm and structured. While when a girl begins to develop into a woman, she begins to develop sex appeal – her face becomes fine, soft and attractive. God placed them there for a purpose. You see that children can play with each other even when they are naked; they will allow you to bath them, but a time will come that when you, as a parent, want to just pick up something in their rooms they will politely ask you to knock before entering their rooms because they have become conscious of themselves. You wonder; what are they trying to cover? Their sexual organs!

It is a normal thing for a married man and his wife to have sex, but it must be within the confines of marriage. Sex outside the bounds of marriage is a sin. Unfortunately, sex has been abused. Companies now use sex appeal to sell their products – cars, pens, microphones, etc., even worse is the movie industry. You'll see a boy and a girl discussing in a scene and the next thing you see is that they have begun to have sex as if it is a normal thing for a boy and a girl to have sex whenever they feel like it. Sex is both physical and spiritual.

Let's look at **1 Cor. 6: 15:**

> *"Do you not know that your bodies are members of Christ? Shall I then take the members of Christ and make them members of a harlot? Certainly not!"*

Anyone who sleeps with a person who they are not married to is sleeping with a harlot. It is sinful to give your body to just anyone. Your body is the temple of the Holy Spirit. Sex is the deepest aspect of marriage, and it is a holy thing. It is supposed to motivate the marriage relationship and love that we are talking about and help the couple bond better. It is the most intimate aspect of marriage. The Bible says Jacob went in to his wife; it is intimate. When you have sex with a harlot (a person who is not your wife), you have messed up your destiny.

1 Cor. 6: 16 says,

> *"Or do you not know that he who is joined to*
> *a harlot is one body with her? For "the two,"*
> *He says, "shall become one flesh."*

If you have sexual intercourse with someone who has misfortune, you become a part of that misfortune. Whatever kind of misfortune the person you are having sex with carries is what you too will carry. Sex is beyond a three-minute activity. When you are joined to a person sexually, you become a partaker of their problems. You automatically take a share in them.

1 Cor. 6: 17 - 20 says,

> *"But he who is joined to the Lord is one*
> *spirit with Him.*
>
> *Flee sexual immorality. Every sin that a man*
> *does is outside the body, but he who commits*
> *sexual immorality sins against his body.*
> *Or do you not know that you body is the*
> *temple of the Holy Spirit who is in you, whom*
> *you have from God, and you are not your*
> *own?*
>
> *For you were bought with a price; therefore*

*glorify God in your body and in your spirit
which are God's."*

You do not belong to yourself; you belong
to God. You have been bought with a price!
Glorify God with your body! How do you
glorify God with your body? By keeping
your body sanctified for him. By waiting
for the man or woman God has prepared for
you. That bone of your bone and flesh of your
flesh. When that man finds you, he would
even be proud of you. You can be bold to tell
your spouse that you reserved yourself for
him or her.

One funny thing about the situation is that
when a man has sex, he can still claim he
never did because there's no way to measure
it. But for a woman, once the hymen is
broken even if it is by accident, how can she
prove that she has not had sex before? Some
men will say, "I will manage and marry you
like that". Sex is more spiritual than it is
physical. It is to bind the husband and the
wife together as one, like glue binds paper
and makes it difficult to tear apart. Scientists
say, although not fully proven, that when a

man is having sexual intercourse with a woman they look at each other, and as they do, some subliminal waves are being transported between the two of them, and that could be traced to why the two begin to look alike after some time.

What we have these days is the reversal of God's order, where 'personal rights' has won out over 'Godly behaviour'. We have 'deified' self and 'humanized' God; thus, bowing down to individualism and free choice. It is now sex before anything else. People now patronise prostitutes for pleasure. Girls now send messages to boys for sex, even in their classrooms. It is amazing to know that a man could pick up any woman on the streets just for sexual pleasure. Some would go to the extent of demanding that the lady must be pregnant before marriage. No! That is not God's order.

PROCREATION

Procreation means having children. God said you would have dominion and multiply and fill the earth. The plan of God is for the man and woman to bring forth their kind to fill the face of the earth through childbearing. These days, more often than not, some people, especially in the western world, decide not to have children; this is actually against God's plan and purpose. That is why you see some countries in the western world giving out visa lotteries so that people could go and fill up their deserted lands. That was what happened to Ireland; at a point they had to make their immigration laws very flexible for people to come in and fill their depopulated land because it was becoming full of old people.

To procreate, according to the dictionary, is to beget or generate offspring; to produce or bring to being. When God created the earth, one of the responsibilities He gave to man was to *"be fruitful, multiply and replenish the earth and subdue it."* **Gen. 2:28**

For God to achieve this through man, He created man and woman that in their fellowship, they will have offspring through which the earth will be multiplied and replenished.

Procreation is one of the primary purposes of marriage, and while it is being given great prominence among men, it is a bi-product of the other reasons for marriage. Procreation or childbearing can only come when there is fellowship between a man and a woman, which results in sex, as children can only come after sex.

However, many go into marriage primarily and for the sole purpose of having children. I have seen would-be couples that decided not to legalize their marriage because the fiancé did not get pregnant; meanwhile, they continue to live in the sin of fornication. Many families have been destroyed because the wife did not conceive. And even while the couple decides to wait till God blesses them, they suffer so much pressure and opposition from their families and friends. Yet, the anxiety to have children, mostly caused by these pressures, has prevented many women from getting pregnant. More so, some of these people applying the pressure never stop to wonder if the couple is even prepared to bring in children yet. They forget that it is not enough to have children, that one must be able to take good care of these children and nurture them for God. If it is delayed, God knows best what is good for us at each point in time.

Mal. 2:15

"And did not he make one? Yet had he the residue of the spirit. And wherefore one? That he might seek a godly seed. Therefore, take heed to your spirit, and let none deal treacherously against the wife of his youth."

God desires godly seed and not seeds that are abused, bent, beaten, and broken. You walk across major cities, and you find children that have become a menace and problem to society. These children came from homes where the parents have failed to train them in the way of the Lord. What is the point of having children that will be a pain to the family and a menace to the society?

Research has shown that most of these children are from dysfunctional homes. Any home where Christ is not the head and in control is most likely to have ungodly children, but when children are trained in the way of the Lord, they are not likely to be wayward.

Companionship comes first before anything else in marriage! When a husband and his wife are in love with each other, they do not need a timetable for sex, it comes naturally to them any day, anytime, anywhere. When you have fellowship and companionship, love will develop, and children will come naturally. Some people do not have children today because of anxiety; setting timetables for sex, all in desperation to have children; thus, tension replaces companionship. They are so desperate to have children that their body chemistry is not sending the right signals. Their body cannot produce children because they are tense. If you are married, relax and enjoy yourself. While you are enjoying yourself, children will come.

Marriage is meant to first mirror the relationship between Christ and the Church, and secondly for companionship; therefore, you must always want to be together. Even when you're far from each other, thank God for telephones, you can call each other as much as you can. Thirdly, it is to satisfy each other sexually. The Bible warns couples not to defraud each other of sex. Do not pretend to be tired or sick because you do not want to have sex with your spouse probably to punish him or her for an offence. Husbands that will not treat their wives well and expect them to give maximum cooperation on the bed are strictly on their own because the women will not be warm and receptive on the bed. Both of you will enjoy it well when you have companionship, and this will bring about procreation.

Chapter Three
God's Own Pattern Of Marriage: The Origin

Marriage is God's creation, as we have established in previous chapters. For the first time since the beginning, it is in the creation of marriage, that we will see God reveal Himself differently, not just as the Creator, but as a Father; He took the role of being the first Father to give away the bride. God made the woman, and then He brought her to Adam, who was oblivious of her creation until she was presented to him. In a profound sense, God had fathered her by virtue of her unique creation, which was quite different from the way the man was created. And although she was designed for Adam, which means he could have just woken up, seen her and taken her, but God, like a Father, 'gave' her to the man in this completely new kind of relationship called marriage; thus marriage is the Father's unique gift to man that reveals His 'Father-God' characteristic, which desires children - godly children who would be every bit like Him.

Let's look at **Gen. 2: 18 – 25:**

> *"And the LORD God said, It is not good that the man should be alone; I will make him an help meet for him.*
>
> *And out of the ground the LORD God formed every beast of the field, and every fowl of the air; and brought them unto Adam to see what he would call them: and whatsoever Adam called every living creature, that was the name thereof.*
>
> *And Adam gave names to all cattle, and to the fowl of the air, and to every beast of the field; but for Adam there was not found an help meet for him.*
>
> *And the LORD God caused a deep sleep to fall upon Adam, and he slept: and he took one of his ribs, and closed up the flesh instead thereof;*
>
> *And the rib, which the LORD God had taken*

from man, made he a woman, and brought her unto the man.

And Adam said, This is now bone of my bones, and flesh of my flesh: she shall be called Woman, because she was taken out of Man.

Therefore shall a man leave his father and his mother and shall cleave unto his wife: and they shall be one flesh.

And they were both naked, the man and his wife, and were not ashamed." (NKJV).

First, it is worthy to note that Adam did not wake up to find the woman sleeping beside him, no; she was properly and respectfully given to him by God the Father; this points to the fact that marriage is designed to follow an order.

God designed marriage as a union between male and female, whom He created in His image and likeness, to be just like Him in every way. He joined them to become one, then blessed them, and empowered their union to be fruitful and multiply, to fill the earth with God-like offspring, and to replenish the earth continually with all things beautiful for the good of man.

Now, let's focus on **verse 18**. In this verse, we see that it was God Himself who decreed that man's solitude is not good, and then by Himself, He sets out to complete one of the central designs of creation, the woman for the man in marriage. Pay attention to the phrase, *"and the Lord God said…"* What is the implication of this? This shows us that God decided all on His own to institute marriage to perfect His creation of the world, without any input from man. Now, don't miss the all-important statement, *"I will make him a helper fit for him;"* God Himself made a human being perfectly suited for the man – a wife.

A partner or helper was not even in Adam's thoughts to start with, not even amongst the animals. Thus, if God had wanted man to marry just anyone, or anything, by all means, He could have made him marry a Peacock, or a Lioness, or any of His special creations, but God didn't do that because that is not His design for marriage. So, He made a declaration that *"it is not good for man to be alone"*, even though Adam never complained he was alone. Hence, it is safe to say that Adam was comfortable with just being with the creatures, as he could communicate perfectly with them *(remember the serpent and the woman spoke to each other – Gen. 3:1-4)*. Besides, it's just like having a dog which has lived with you for years, all you need to do is make a sign or speak, and it would understand what you are trying to communicate to it. So, Adam, I believe, was quite comfortable with the animals, but God still said that Adam was alone. Being the all-wise and all-knowing God, He saw what Adam could not yet comprehend: He saw that man had a problem that needed urgent attention.

LONELINESS

Critically examining **verse 18**, we see that man did not realise he had a problem. He did not even understand what the feeling of loneliness was, even though he may have been experiencing it. However, God stepped in because He understood what the man was going through even when Adam could not explain it. The scripture in **Heb.4:15a** explains this further:

"For we do not have a high priest who is unable to empathise with our weaknesses"

We have established that God was the one who discovered the problem of man's loneliness. Someone can be in a noisy crowd and still be super lonely. Thus, God solved the problem of man that He discovered. So, you can't just wake up one morning and decide to be married; God needs to help you with that. He caused a deep sleep to fall on Adam and brought out a rib from his side from which He made the woman. Why not another man? Why Eve and not Steve? No! Adam needed a look-alike with a womb!

More often than not, every mature man or woman who is not married has a problem of loneliness, whether or not he or she admits it is irrelevant. You need a spouse. Some of the clues to know this bone of your bone when you meet him or her is you would always want to be around each other, if the persons are naturally quiet, they become talkative around each other, and they love each other genuinely, not lust.

It is not good for a man to be alone. Loneliness is what makes a man go straight to the beer parlour after work instead of going home. For a lonely Christian brother, you'll find him at all of the Church's fellowship; even when the meeting is for teenagers and children, you will find him there trying to kill his loneliness and kill time. But if a married man prefers to go to the beer parlour from work, then there is a problem in his home. One of the signs to use to identify a home with a problem of loneliness is when a couple no longer desires the company of each other again.

Some time ago, I went to check on one of my friends; we were childhood friends. This man and his wife started dating while they were still in secondary school, and they have children now. I got to their home and was told he was not at home. However, I was baffled when his wife wished aloud that he should not return home early. So, I questioned her. All she could say was that the matter between them was a very long story.

No man is complete without a wife. Marriage is the best thing that can happen to you when you marry the one God has ordained for you. Your life would be easy, and things would work for you because you have the backing of God. Even when there are challenges, your marriage will thrive.

DATING AND COURTSHIP

In Christendom, we do not practice dating. What we practice is courtship because the latter is well defined from the outset. What is dating? Dating means to test and see if this relationship will work or not. It encourages the couple to engage in ungodly acts like kissing, sex, and even cohabiting. The couple date to know how far they can take the relationship. Some will even date to know if they are sexually compatible with their partner. If not, they move on to the next person until the number is countless. It is like a butterfly trying to taste different flowers. Some men will sample as many city girls as they could and then go to their village to pick a wife when it's time. Courtship, on the other hand is godly. Courtship is the period the intending partners are waiting to formalise their marriage plans, having been confirmed as fit to be married, after following the laid down procedure by the local Church.

WHAT NOT TO CONSIDER IN A POTENTIAL SPOUSE

1. **Do not look at the physical appearance:** A lot of us have our mindsets. Many people look out for the physical appearance of a person first (tall, dark, short, skin complexion, etc). These attributes should not be the basis for finding a partner because those things will surely disappear. Before I married my wife, I had full hair, so I kept an afro. But today, my hair is gradually receding. So, if you married a man because of the afro he keeps, and he becomes bald after some years, will you divorce him? Some ladies would rather marry a handsome man even if he didn't have a kobo to his name. They don't care if he has a bank account or not, as long as he is good looking and presentable. They would do anything within their reach to be with that man. What if that man has an accident and

gets deformed? Will such ladies still continue with the marriage?

I accosted a man as he was assaulting his wife because she had grown bigger. He complained that when he married her at twenty-two, she was very slim and was a figure-eight in shape. Now, at forty-two, after having three children, she no longer looks like the woman he married, and so he became angry and beat her up. Can you imagine! Physical appearance will change with age and so it must not be the basis for making your choice of marriage partner.

2. **Do not marry a person because of his or her societal or financial status:**
Do not marry a person for their status because that status can change within a split second. Wealth can vanish, business can get bankrupt, political status may change if they lose an election, there can be a loss of job, and so on. It takes just one event to cause either a positive or negative change in the life of that person. If you marry a man because he is a king in the making and after a few months of marriage, he dies, and some other person takes his place, what

would you do? The problem starts with your mind; you have an idea of how you want your life to be. It is a dream and there is nothing wrong in dreaming but submit your dreams to God and do not struggle with Him in your choices. Change your mindset and let God take charge.

3. **Do not choose a person whom God is not leading you to marry:**

Do not marry a person who does not speak the same spiritual language with you. Can two walk together unless they agree? (Amos 3:3). Both individuals must feel like their relationship brings them closer to Jesus. Without Jesus, a couple will most likely not survive the storms and struggles that are a part of marriage. The only reason why you must get married should be because you are being led by God to marry that person. That is why when a couple comes to me, I ask them critical questions about their convictions. If they insist God is leading them, I also will inquire of God to know. If God tells me otherwise, I will counsel the pair that the marriage should not hold. However, if they insist, they can go to another Church and get married, but I will give them the right counsel. Jesus must be the rock on which your marriage is standing. So, you must start with Jesus by praying and watching. Be careful with your dreams also. Dreams are good but sometimes really deceptive. You may pray for a sign, and then you get one and make your decisions based on them. For instance, you see yourself cutting a stick in your dreams with a blunt knife, and all of a sudden, a man comes to you with a new sharp knife, and the stick begins to cut. Or you are drawing water from a well, and then he comes to help you with it. It is not always like that. These are the stories we hear every day.

You need to have an inner peace that is given only by God concerning that person. Many of us do not have a relationship with God, but when it's time for marriage, we would want to hear from Him. If God is not involved in your daily life and does not speak to you about other little things; when you present weightier matters, it becomes very difficult for you to understand His voice. This is the reason why some people will tell you God has shown them two or three people at the same time as their spouse. God is not an author of confusion; thus, He will never show you more than one person to be your spouse.

Someone once came to me with two ladies that God said were his wife, but he was confused about whom to pick. I told him straight that God hadn't spoken to him. God is not like that! When God created Adam and decided it was time to get him his wife, He presented one woman to him. He didn't have to gamble on the choice of his wife! Meaning, you have the bone of your bone and flesh of your flesh out there; stop gambling about it. You need to find her, and you will find her in the place of prayers.

4. **Start early**
You do not begin to pray for your spouse when you think you are ready to get married. Start early. Start preparing and praying about it now. If you want to become an engineer, you start preparing from primary school. By the time you get to secondary school, you select the right subjects that would further birth that dream, not the opposite. If not, your dream of becoming an engineer will never materialise.

Likewise, if you are aged twenty already, especially if you are a lady, you can get married anytime from now. Also, I often encourage parents to pray for their children's spouses from a very tender age. Even right from the womb! As a parent, you may have a fantastic home, and one boy or girl will just come from nowhere and destroy a home you have been building for thirty years all in the name of a son-in-law or daughter-in-law. Even your future in-law are subject to prayers, so pray about them. You can never go wrong with prayers.

Summarily, our Father, God, always wants to give us the best, especially in marriage, but ever so often, man never comprehends what is good for him, and thus, blindly defies and abuses that which is meant to be for his good, as marriage is abused today. After the fall, the first man, Adam, was the first to abuse marriage. Adam became so defiant and careless, which was evident in his response when God questioned him about what he had done; he said, *"the woman whom YOU gave me caused me to do this"* (**Gen.3:12**). Rather than apologise and let the all-wise God make things right again, Adam blamed the Father for giving him a good thing, which he mismanaged all by himself. Yes, Adam mismanaged his marriage by sitting back and letting his woman take the lead, enough to convince him to take the wrong way on 'an instruction' He was clearly given by God, instead of leading her as 'the head' of the union. Adam was the only one to whom God gave the instruction 'directly' not to eat the fruit of that tree because he was the vision-carrier of the home, who was then expected to instruct and guide the woman; thus, lead her in the right way of the vision, so that she can help him effectively in the pursuit of his God-given vision. God never gave the woman that instruction directly, only the man. We can see this in these two scriptures: Gen. 2:16 and Gen. 3:17.

Gen. 2:16:

"And the Lord God commanded the man, "You are free to eat from any tree in the garden; but you must not eat from the tree of the knowledge of good and evil, for when you eat from it you will certainly die."

Gen. 3:17:

"Then to Adam He said, "Because you

have listened to the voice of your wife, and have eaten from the tree about which I commanded you, saying, 'You shall not eat from it'; Cursed is the ground because of you; In toil you shall eat of it All the days of your life."

However, even the mismanagement, the fall, and the defiance of man did not, has not, and will not change the plan of God for marriage. Marriage is patterned after Christ, putting the man in the lead, not the woman. So, to turn it the other way around is gross mismanagement, and then the marriage becomes what it was not intended to be. This is the more reason if our marriages must work, we then must be rooted in the originator, God, and follow His instructions.

Chapter Four
A Helper Comparable

God designed the husband and wife to fit together in a way that creates unity and strength in a marriage; thus, create a home instead of just a house people exist in. It's the same complementary nature that happens when two parts of a thing fit together to work as one. Similarly, just as God designed the husband to step into the marriage with love and leadership to meet the needs the wife cannot meet on her own, He also created the wife to step into the marriage with honour and respect to meet her husband's needs and help with what the husband is not able to accomplish alone. Only the wife can fill this role, and when she does, she completes the husband and experiences a deeper level of fulfilment because God has given them both complementary roles that are neither superior nor inferior to each other but working in sync with one another. The roles are not designed to be reversed. You see, when God made ready a bride for his son, Adam, He did not make just any woman for him as long as she could bear children. No! He was very deliberate about the kind of woman He was preparing for him. He made him a helper comparable to him. Not just a helper but one that is comparable; that is what makes it possible for husband and wife to fit together as one and complement each other to make the marriage become what God intended.

Let's take a look at **Gen: 2:18**,

> *"And the LORD God said, It is not good that the man should be alone; I will make him an helper comparable to him."* (NKJV)

Let's also see how the Amplified version puts **Gen. 2:18:**

> *"Now the Lord God said, "It is not good (beneficial) for the man to be alone; I will make him a helper [one who balances*

him—a counterpart who is] suitable and complementary for him. (Amp)

God did not just stop at making a helper for the man, but He made him a helper that balances him, a counterpart that fits him correctly. The point is anybody can help you, but not just anybody can be that comparable help who balances you. Somebody can help you to destroy yourself or your vision; yet, bad as it may seem, that person has helped you. God gave Adam a helper comparable to him; a counterpart who understands and supports the vision to help him bring it to fruition, with him taking the lead, instructing her on the expectations and boundaries of the vision, not too busy or unmindful, as to leave the leadership role to her. When the husband is effective in his leadership role, his priorities will shape the wife's approach, where she becomes positively helpful, a champion for her husband, nurturer of their children, and mentor for younger women, influencing the world positively. This is critical, and it explains why a good wife is so highly valued in the Bible, as we see in **Prov. 31:10-12:**

An excellent wife, who can find? For her worth is far above jewels.
The heart of her husband trusts in her, and he will have no lack of gain.
She does him good and not evil all the days of her life.

The heart of her husband can trust her and feed off the support of his wife because he leads her well, not as someone inferior to him, but as a counterpart excellent for him. We all have our insecurities, but it is even worse for a man; sometimes, he fears about how things may play out when pressure mounts and his position as a man is threatened. One of his greatest fear is to lose respect and honour in his own home. A wife's support, both in action and words, gives the husband strength, as they work together to figure it out. A wife is a powerful influence in the family, and when she is committed to the cause and tells her husband, *"this is possible, we can do this,"* she becomes the glue that holds everything together, as God intended her to be. The wife's role is a divine call to honour and to affirm her husband's leadership and help carry it through according to her gifts, which matches the needs of his vision and purpose. Now, that is another reason to be careful who you marry; she can make or break you.

Moreover, it is vital to understand that to work together and achieve great results in the world through the family unit is a significant part of the reason the Lord God said it is not good (not beneficial) for the man to be alone! That is why who you marry is important, and also why you cannot remain alone after a certain age. If you are age thirty as a man and you are not thinking of marriage, begin to have a rethink. If you are a woman of marriageable age and no one is coming, I decree that this year, God shall settle you, in Jesus' name! Amen.

Some men of marriageable age are the cause of their loneliness because they still want to enjoy life; but when you see the bone of your bone that idea drops away. For instance, before I met my wife, I had plans for myself. I dreamed that at age thirty I would have made much money, bought the reigning car then (Volvo) and cruised around town in nice singlet and knickers from one Beer parlour to another with different girls. But when I met my wife, all those concepts faded away. Although I was not godly then, we still had to work out our relationship. Thank God for what we have today.

Many people have missed their right spouses because they have refused to think rightly. They have messed up the lives of genuine people God had brought to them who could have been perfect spouses because they choose not to be godly and focused. After these good people must have waited a long time for them to do the right thing, and without positive responses, they left them for some other persons who were ready. They refused to do what God wanted them to do. As a person, if your relationship with God is right, you will never make mistake in your choice of a life partner.

The New International Version (NIV) says, *"a helper suitable for him"*. What does that mean? It means that the helper has met all the criteria and is satisfactory or perfect for him. A helper that has met all the requirements needed to help you fulfil your life given purpose. God has a woman or man out there that He has specially prepared with everything necessary to help you fulfil your purpose. It is only a suitable wife that can submit to her husband and take the blame even when he is the one at fault. When something is suitable, it is ideal; it matches, it is a perfect fit, it is adaptable, and it is complementary. This means that the woman completes him because the man is not complete without her.

Back in the days, when I used to visit the cinema a lot, I enjoyed seeing Indian movies. In one of those movies I saw then, a group of gangsters was to deliver a parcel of hard drugs from one city to another. For them to be able to identify their client, the dealers needed to roughly cut into two One Rupee note, which was like a Dollar bill and gave their client the other half. At the point of delivery, the client would bring out the other part of the currency note to match with that of the delivery man. If it doesn't match there would not be a delivery. It must match.

Let's look at another version, the New Living Translation - **Gen. 2:18**,

"And the LORD God said, it is not good that the man should be alone; I will make him a helper who is just right for him."

God saved me from marrying the wrong woman because He saw my future and brought me my wife. When I married my wife, I was a drunkard, womanizer, and a chain smoker, but God saw my future. If I had married someone else, my ministry would not have seen the light of day. God gave me a woman who could accommodate me and all my excesses; she has the shock absorber to bear anything that is thrown at her. My wife is one person that would leave her room to entertain a guest even when she is too tired or sleepy. You'd be really fortunate when you come to our house when I am the only one at home, and I remember to offer you a glass of water. It's not what I would ordinarily think to do, but it's her default mode. God knew that she was just right for me.

If you have prayed and heard God clearly about your wife and you are sure of it, then that is great. If you go ahead and marry her, and come back after ten years to declare that she is a useless wife and no-good woman, check yourself very well, it is you that has a problem, not her because God gave you a wife that is just right. When God gives you a wife, He gives you a helper comparable: a perfect one. So, you don't just wake up one morning and decide to pick just anyone to call your wife. Maybe to you, your ideal wife must be someone very beautiful and you know where to find her, at the club. Well, congratulations in advance on your marriage to her. Alternatively, maybe you are waiting to go to the village for Christmas to pick a bride; you may end up with a puzzle that would wreck your destiny because every girl of marriageable age would be in her best behaviour then. However, the truth is, if God gives you your wife, you can go to sleep without fear. That does not mean that there would not be quarrels, but those quarrels are to strengthen the bond.

I see some men fighting their wives for not washing their clothes or cooking their food at a particular time. Did you marry a cook? Is she your laundry woman? Actually, let's get real now, it is your duty as a man to love her enough to wash yours and hers, provide the food, cook it and invite her to the table often, because she is your help meet not your house-help, nanny or slave. She is the daughter of the Most-High King and must be treated as such.

Also, as a helper, if the responsibility given to your husband fails in his hands, you'd be held responsible by God because He knew that the man would not have been able to bear the responsibility alone and that was why He sent you to him. So, if you know what he needs or what you need to do to help him succeed, do it. If he needs food or a warm bath after a hard day's work, make them ready! As a wife, you bear the greatest responsibility. The man's success is your responsibility; make no mistake about that.

You would notice that when man fell in the Garden of Eden, the serpent was cursed directly, the woman was also cursed directly, but the man was not directly cursed, that would have destroyed or nullified the whole design of God for the marriage institution, having designed the man as the head of the union, which represents Christ and the Church. Instead, the ground was cursed on his behalf because the woman was specially designed to help Adam fulfil his purpose successfully, but she derailed him from it, just as Paul points out in **1 Timothy 2:14**, *"And Adam was not the one deceived; it was the woman who was deceived and became a sinner."*

However, we get more clarity on the curse in **Gen. 3:17:**

> *"Then to Adam He said, "Because you have listened to the voice of your wife, and have eaten from the tree about which I commanded you, saying, 'You shall not eat from it'; Cursed is the ground because of you; In toil you shall eat of it All the days of your life."*

Firstly, before we go further, let me explain the context of this scripture, the 'ground' here is not referring to the whole earth or that God had cursed all grounds in the world for man, as many tend to believe. According to Strong's Bible Concordance H127, the Hebrew word *"adamah"* is not commonly translated "ground." In fact, the most common translation is "land." Therefore, the most likely meaning of the verse is about the geographic area of the man's service, which for Adam, was the Garden of Eden, the place where he carried out his God-given purpose. 'Cursed ground' was not referring to all grounds in general, but to the man's specific place of 'purpose' or operation that brings them both the kind of fulfilment that nothing else can offer.

Evidently, the man and the woman are a team designed for purpose unto fulfilment, and the woman is to help him deliver it successfully in the ways that God has gifted her to suit his specific office. Consequently, when the woman does not do her part effectively, and the man fails in this duty, she suffers the most. The man takes out his frustrations on her and points the accusing finger at her for his failures and struggles, even though she may know nothing about it. It is a natural default mode because of her divine design as the man's helper. That is why in God's design, there's nothing like divorce because you can't get the work done alone. When God gave you your wife, He gave you His best, the bone of your bone. And you cannot say she is your "bone" therefore you have the right to remove (divorce) her because you have problems with her. Your union, with all of its problems, is not a medical condition that require 'physical' surgery or removal of the part inconveniencing you; it is a spiritual covenant that cannot be put asunder or separated by anyone, not even you or your spouse, and thus, it is too late. So, rather than put two of you asunder, take that problem to God; you can still take that failing marriage to God in prayer because He started it, and He will sort out any challenges in the family.

Looking at the love relationship between Jesus and the Church, His bride, we find that this is the standard expected of every marriage: man is to love his wife as Christ loved the Church. The beauty is that the relationship between Christ and the Church is perfect; no matter what is going on in the Church today, Christ still loves her. He has paid the ultimate price for her; He cannot reject the Church; He cannot despise the Church; He cannot divorce her. No matter what is happening, He will come back to take the Church home. So, you too should not reject your wife, neither should you despise nor divorce her. It would be best for you to embrace her and work together to make it right. It is not good for a man to live alone. God does not make mistakes neither does He do anything by accident.

For every marriage that has been contracted today, God is aware. He allowed it for His purpose – that He may be glorified. Whatever it is that is happening today in your home that is making you fight each other, you need to know it is caused by a common enemy, the devil; so, stop seeing your spouse as your enemy. Gen. 3, talks about a visitor to the Garden. Who was the visitor? It was the devil, speaking through the snake. The Devil is always there to destroy the home because he knows that God has a special plan for every home. It is wise to recognise his antics and stop him right on time.

Chapter Five
Prerequisite For Harmony In The Home

The good news is that God designed marriage to be both harmonious and holy; to be the deepest and most fulfilling relationship on earth. And it can be. But how? What are the things we need to do to bring the kind of unity and peace that God wants in the home? The prerequisites for a great marriage are in the heart of God and revealed through His Word. All that we need to do can be found in the passages we have been studying so far. However, we must first understand that even the best of marriages requires hard work, no exceptions. To live harmoniously with another person is a daily process that demands unselfishness and calls for love without conditions because every marriage is intended to be a continual work in progress. So, don't begin to imagine that it is your husband or wife that is the cause of the problems in your marriage. Instead, be wise to see it as God opening your eyes to the weak points in your marriage that needs to be worked on, and also your personal weaknesses you both need to address gracefully, without judging and condemning each other.

In addressing some of these problems, where you discover your wrongdoing, you may need to go on your knees to apologise to your spouse; do not hesitate to do that. Sincerely, it is not a wrong thing for couples to kneel for each other to apologise when they are wrong. A man who cannot kneel for his wife to apologise when he is wrong is heading for destruction; that act of pride alone can send him to hell. Take, for instance, that on a Sunday morning as I prepare for Church to go and preach the Word of God, my wife locks the door and says that I'm not going anywhere. What do you think I would do? I will humbly kneel before her and plead with her and ask her to forgive me for whatever I must have done. I won't allow pride to get in the way.

Some time ago, I was talking to a couple who were having serious problems in their marriage. I took the man aside and explained the need to help his wife at home. I went further to tell him that I even wash my wife's underwear. He was dazed and vehemently responded that he would never do such a thing. But his wife can and does wash his.

Let's be real! If your wife is in the kitchen cooking, then racing in and out to attend to the baby crying at one end of the room, with her underwears soaked ready for washing in the bathroom, then you go in for a bath and leave afterwards. Would you pretend not to see those soaked clothes? As if leaving her alone to all the chores is not enough, by the time she gets to the bathroom, she finds that you've left your own underpants and singlet waiting for her to wash, and worse still, you did not make an effort to soak yours to make the process easy for her. How do you think she would feel? Put yourself in her shoes, how would you feel? Then you will come back two days later to ask her for those same underpants. Unbelievable! If I were her, I would tell you that your underpants and singlet are inside the water. This woman has come to help you, don't be so proud and thoughtless; help her to be more productive and useful to you.

Let's look at **Gen. 2: 18 – 20,**

> *"And the LORD God said, It is not good that the man should be alone; I will make him an helper comparable to him.*
>
> *And out of the ground the LORD God formed every beast of the field, and every fowl of the air; and brought them unto Adam to see what he would call them: and whatsoever Adam called every living creature, that was the name thereof.*
>
> *And Adam gave names to all cattle, and to the fowl of the air, and to every beast of the field; but for Adam there was not found an help meet for him."* (NKJV)

God has given man everything: dominion and authority over everything. But the Bible says that there was no helper comparable to him! He considered everything He created - the animals, the birds, etc., and there was not found a helper suitable, perfect or just right for him. None was complimentary or adaptive enough to him. God knew that man needed somebody just like him; thus, He gave the woman to man. Make no mistake about it, God did not provide a housemaid for the man; He gave the man a perfect match to complete him for the work he has been assigned. You see, God, in His infinite wisdom, knew that the man, Adam, needed help for all that work to tend to the Garden of Eden and all its inhabitants; it was much work, and there was no way Adam alone would be able to accomplish all that on his own without a good support system, who is as intelligent as he is and not less than him, to work side by side 'with him' to 'help' him fulfill the assignment. God made your wife a helper that would help you fulfill His purpose for your life; she is not to be treated like your servant, she is to be treated like 'you' because, by God's design, she is 'you' – you are one. The command is, love your wife as Christ loves the Church.

Gen. 2:21-25 states,

"And the LORD God caused a deep sleep to fall upon Adam, and he slept: and he took

one of his ribs, and closed up the flesh instead thereof;

And the rib, which the LORD God had taken from man, made he a woman, and brought her unto the man.

And Adam said, This is now bone of my bones, and flesh of my flesh: she shall be called Woman, because she was taken out of Man.

Therefore shall a man leave his father and his mother, and shall cleave unto his wife: and they shall be one flesh.

And they were both naked, the man and his wife, and were not ashamed. (NKJV)

The plan of God is not for us to be having fights, quarrels, and being thoughtless and inconsiderate of each other in our homes. Marriage is supposed to bring a better life to you; it is supposed to lead you closer to God. Your home is supposed to be as sweet as it was in the Garden of Eden when God created it without sin. When your entire family understands the core message of the teaching, everyone will know what he or she is required to do to make the home what it ought to be.

WHAT ARE THE PREREQUISITES FOR MARRIAGE?

According to the Advanced Learners English dictionary, prerequisites are the things which must exist or happen before something else can exist or happen. Below is a list of prerequisites for harmony in the home:

Spiritual Unity

2 Cor. 6:14,

> *"Be ye not unequally yoked together with unbelievers: for what fellowship hath righteousness with unrighteousness? And what communion hath light with darkness?"* (NKJV)

It means the husband and the wife must be born again. They must be regenerated. They must have the same focus when it comes to God. They must be drinking from the same spiritual cup. They must attend the same Church to avoid unnecessary confusions and conflicting ideologies. The husband cannot be a Baptist while the wife is a Methodist. That will cause confusion in the house because they will not hear the same message.

116

What if their pastors do not have a clear understanding when it comes to issues of marriage or important family issues? What if their own homes are probably not even in right standing, so they don't even have the boldness to preach or teach such messages in the Church because they know if they do that their members will question their authority?

Some pastors would even encourage members to marry spouses from other religions as long as the person has money or is good looking. They don't mind or care about their faith or spiritual status. They will tell their sisters, especially that "if he must marry you, he must have a house, a car and be working in a good place" and so on. They will tell her "don't marry and begin to suffer!"

Can I tell you something? He doesn't need to have a house, but he needs to have a home where both of you will live. He doesn't have to have a car; a car will come as both of you work together to build your home and strive to fulfill your purpose. When I started my life with my wife, we had a beautiful large sitting room. It was empty. We had no furniture except a small wooden chair that is used in the kitchen when cooking, a ceiling fan, and a mattress which was in the bedroom. In the afternoon, we played in the sitting room, but at night we bring our mattress to the sitting room to sleep under the only fan we had in the house.

One day, a friend of mine came to our house with a football. So, I asked him, "what are you coming to do with a football here?" And he said he came to play football in my sitting room. Is my house a stadium? I wondered, shaking my head and laughing. Our house was literally empty, but we made sure that the kitchen was well equipped. That was my wife's office, as she would call it. We had a cooker, a stove and a small fridge. In fact, the fridge we had was the fridge my wife used when she was in school. So, if you want the man to have everything you might be quite mistaken. Today, we live in a house that has five bedrooms, and those rooms are unable to contain all that we have. When you come to our compound, you find a lot of things around that have no place in the house; we give out most of them to people. I had no car when we got married but between then and now, I have given out five cars.

If you judge a person's future by their present situation, you might be making a huge mistake. If you despise their future because of what you see today, you might just be despising your own future. If God tells you that this person is your future wife or husband and you despise him or her God will substitute you and by the time you meet that person in the future, you may be full of regrets.

When I met my wife, I had only one pair of shoes, but today if I want to wear ten shoes in one day I can. These are serious matters. What we took into our marriage was hope! My beginning may have been small, but my end shall be great. If you look at that brother now and despise him, you despise his God! And his God will yet arise for him and make him what He wants him to be. But by then you will not be a partaker of it. You will only be watching as a spectator, wishing that you had acted differently. But if wishes were horses, even beggars would ride.

119

Also, if you marry a spouse who is not of the same spiritual frequency with you or genuinely born again, that person will pull you down. For instance, my wife and I were unbelievers when we got married, but when she became born again, she prayed a lot for my salvation. Back then I used to question her saying, "were you the one that killed Jesus?" And I would move my things out of the bedroom and sleep in the sitting room because I know the bedroom belongs to her as well.

One fateful day, two of her pastors came to our house, I was in my sitting room, and I was drinking beer with fish. So, she heard them knock downstairs, we were upstairs, and she came to me agitated, to say that her Church leaders were around. My response to her was that if they want to come and drink beer with me, they could come and have some. Do you know why I responded that way to her? We were not operating on the same frequency. When you and your spouse are not operating in spiritual unity, you can't move forward because, first of all, you are not in agreement spiritually. The Bible says, if two of you shall agree on anything, it shall be done unto you. If you can't agree spiritually, you both struggle on everything.

The agreement between the husband and the wife is the most potent agreement. Take for instance, if my son and the son of my Assistant Pastor both apply for a particular scholarship meant for only one person, and my Assistant Pastor comes to me for us to agree in prayers for his son to get that scholarship. I will only pray a generic prayer of thanksgiving with him because I also want my son to get that scholarship. But if he and his wife hold hands in agreement, their focus is the same, God will answer them. The two of you must be pursuing God together; it's absolutely important. When God brought you into your spouse's life, He had a purpose. And that purpose of God must be fulfilled. That purpose must be a priority, even when it is not convenient or when you feel cheated. In your marriage, make it your goal to please God.

A godly woman submits to her husband. An unbelieving wife will not submit to her husband because she may not be accountable to anybody. An ungodly wife will rub in her husband's inadequacies on him, especially when she is the one that provides for the family. I have witnessed this scenario before. The man and his wife had a disagreement, and she threw him out of the house because she pays the rent. After they settled their dispute, the man vowed never to go back to that house; he forgave her but told her that they would only come to live together under one roof when he has money to rent a house. The desire to please God in all things will inspire the couple to please each other in all respect. Let's take a look at this diagram:

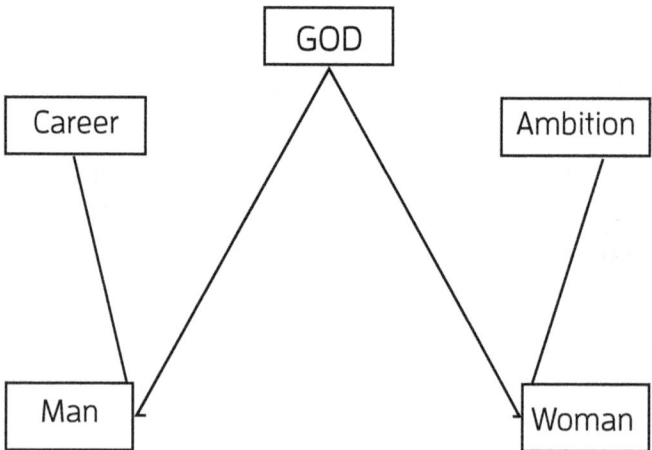

We see God above in the diagram. The man and his wife are opposite each other. If the husband is pursuing money and the wife is pursuing ambition, you see both of them moving far away from each other; they can never meet. And if one is pursuing God and the other is chasing after something else, they can never meet. At the points when both of them start pursuing God, the gap begins to narrow, and then there is a meeting point. The truth is that there will always be issues in marriage if the gap is not covered, but when you pursue God, He reveals to you the purpose of your marriage. The more both of you pursue God, the closer you get to each other, even when it is tough to get to the main point, grace will carry you there. If you do not have Jesus in your life, you operate in a general form of grace and find yourselves at cross purposes.

Regenerated people rely on God to make their home a replica of heaven on earth. A regenerated man loves his spouse even at the expense of his own comfort. Sacrifice yourself for your spouse; love your spouse unconditionally just as Jesus loves the

Church. He loves the Church so much that He gave his life for her. Go back to the Love letters you wrote to each other before you got married. What went wrong? While we were yet sinners, Christ loved and died for us. When you and your spouse are not reaching an agreement, and you know the decision he or she wants to take will surely create problems for the family, do not continue to argue with him or her, take the matter to God and present your strong reasons. Remember the Bible says in **Prov. 21:1,**

"The king's heart is in the hand of the Lord, as the rivers of water: he turneth it withersoever he will." (KJV)

If that decision is not correct, God will change his heart. Obedience is key. If you marry an unbeliever who is going to hell, he or she will make sure he or she drags you along with him. If a man's physical appearance and eloquence are the reasons why you got married to him, when you get into his house, you will realize that you have married the devil's incarnate. If you marry an unbeliever, until he repents, you have the devil as your father-in-law. We all know the devil has just three missions; to steal, to kill and to destroy. Be wise and choose wisely.

Accept Each Other.
You must learn to accept each other bearing in mind that the two of you are from different backgrounds. Acceptance here means wholehearted commitment and absolute loyalty to the person with all of his or her weaknesses and strengths as is, understanding you didn't marry your spouse because he or she is perfect, in the first place, but because you gave each other a covenant promise of love without conditions and to cleave as one; that promise makes up for each of your faults. I will give an example. My father was a Policeman, and then he resigned and became a Court Clerk, and from there became a businessman, a politician and a polygamist. My mother was a stack illiterate. You can imagine my background. Now, the woman whom I married has both parents as teachers, who trained their children strictly and with a good educational foundation. In my days in primary and secondary school, teacher's children were the most intelligent; I don't

125

know about now. They came to school very neat, and they live their lives as though they were not living in the same world with the rest of us.

Her father had just one wife - her mother, while my father had three and a half wives (the fourth attempt to marry another woman failed because she left the marriage early). Thus, my wife and I had totally opposite backgrounds. So, how do we merge our ideologies and have a common ground? My wife is not as organized as I am. In the early years of our marriage, immediately we return home from Church, the first place she goes to was the kitchen. As she goes in, she will remove and leave her shoes in the sitting room, her hat in the kitchen, and she may change her clothes and leave it scattered everywhere in the bedroom, or she will just remain in that same clothes all day. I would almost shout my heart out because it irritated me so much. Sometimes, she moves my things and I would have to search for a while to find them. After some years, living with her, I eventually learnt to understand her, when I did, I began to help organize her things, so we can both remain sane. However, when it comes to finances, she is very detailed and meticulous in her spending, while I spend money anyhow. Ask her of any money given to her months or years back, and she would give you a detailed account of how she spent every dime.

The first quarrel I had with my wife was way back in school in 1983 while we were still courting, and a hundred naira caused it. We used to have a joint pocket, like a joint account, and I collected a hundred naira from it to go to the city of Ibadan. So, I travelled and returned to school at 6:00pm same day. At about 8:00pm, my wife came to visit me and asked about my whereabouts. I told her about my trip, and even gave details of the money I had taken and precisely how I spent forty Naira out of it. My wife broke down in tears; she considered my spending extravagant because usually, forty-five Naira could sustain a student in a month, and I had spent forty Naira in two hours. That day wasn't funny, but it helped me learn a crucial life lesson, and gradually, we began to understand each other, and each began to adjust. God knew I needed a help meet that would help curtail

127

and channel my spending right. Today, I don't even buy things by myself because I may not be able to give a proper account. So, if I need anything, I give her the money to get them for me. If she is helping me to organize my finances, then I ought to help her organize herself. Thus, this is how we can complement each other as a couple to achieve God's purpose for our marriage.

Let's reason this hypothetical situation together. If the morning after your wedding night you woke up feeling a cold sensation on your body – your wife has bed-wetted, what would you do? Would you scold her or help her overcome it? What if you discovered that she didn't know how to cook? I know of a couple who met during their NYSC year. The woman didn't know how to cook. If she even boils water the pot would dry up and burn. But the man had to train her patiently. Today, she cooks so well that whenever I visit them, the only thing I request for is *Isi-Ewu*. A woman who could not boil water successfully is now cooking *Isi-Ewu*. It means she has a teachable heart; her husband accepted her, and she learnt. Likewise, one of my sisters who got married to an Ijesha man, could not pound yam, and that is the main food of the Ijeshas. But then, this man would go into the kitchen with her, shut the door behind them and pound yam for everyone, including their guest. He never condemned her, and nobody knew until they told them. Today, she can pound yam for as many people as possible. She has learnt, and they have a wonderful home.

God never created any two people the same. That is why when your biometrics are taken, your thumb prints and your eyes are very important because no two people have the same. We are not the same, but once we are married, we gradually grow to become one, completing each other.

How can we now live together if we are not the same?

Many of us come into the marriage with a fixed mindset, garbage, and whatever we have learnt from our different backgrounds. Our attitude and response to issues are controlled and influenced by such things; thus, for couples to live together harmoniously; they must first purge themselves of all these things and take up the mind of Christ. That can only be accomplished by the power of the Holy Spirit, if and when we surrender our lives to the authority of our Lord Jesus Christ.

Phil.3:16 says,

"Nevertheless, to the degree that we have already attained, let us walk by the same rule, let us be of the same mind.

We can only walk by the same rule and be of the same mind if we first surrender our different attributes and take up one that is common to us and agree to submit ourselves to each other.

Phil. 2:5 says,

"Let this mind be in you, which was also in Christ Jesus:"

We must take up the mind of Christ, which is love, humility, faith, gentleness, self-control, goodness, longsuffering forgiveness, and peace.

That means that the two of you must submit

yourselves at the altar of Christ. Put down your ideas, achievements, pride and all at the altar of Christ and take up His mind. The mind of Christ is sacrificial and selfless, accepting a sinner just the way he or she comes. For two of you to walk together, you must mind the same things. So, God brought you together to help complement each other's good attributes and eliminate each other's wrong attributes. The content of a bottle of Coke has a dark colour. How do you make it pure? You open it up to a tap flowing with clean water, and after a while, the bottle will only contain pure content. When you submit to Christ, the Spirit of God will flush out the works of the flesh from you and you would get to a point where you discover that you've lost appetite for the sins you used to commit. You cannot change any man. We were all created in a peculiar way; accept the personality of your spouse.

Gen. 2:22 - 23 says,
> *"And the rib, which the LORD God had taken from man, made he a woman, and brought her unto the man.*
> *And Adam said, This is now bone of my*

bones, and flesh of my flesh: she shall be called Woman, because she was taken out of Man. (NKJV)

Adam did not complain; he accepted the woman brought to him. There's somebody that God has created for you and He will bring that person at the right time. How do you now get connected to that person? You get connected to them on your knees through prayer. Many people begin to pray for their spouse when they feel it's time for them to get married. Parents, pray for the spouses of your children now that they are still young!

My wife told me a story about her mother – my mother-in-law. My mother-in-law lost her own mother at a very young age; thus, she was ill-treated by her father's wives. On the eve of her wedding, she locked herself in a room and went to God in prayers, covenanting herself and her seeds to God. She prayed to God that if the children He would give her would end up becoming a menace to the society, that God should not give her any. She also prayed for the longevity of life to train all her children until they could stand on their own. God answered her prayers; all her sons are pastors today and one of her two daughters is married to a pastor. At the airport, on her return from one of her visits to one of her sons in the United States, she told God that He could take her life from then because her eyes had seen His goodness on all her children.

Openness

Gen. 2: 25,

"And they were both naked, the man and his wife, and were not ashamed. (NKJV)

The above verse is an offshoot of Verse 24, where the two cleave in a one-flesh union; thus, creating the relationship where verse 25 can happen. The covenant relationship established by marriage is designed from the beginning to be the main foundation of freedom from shame because marriage is the only grounds a man and a woman have full rights with God's backing to be totally naked with each other, and not be judged.

Moreover, the very essence of this covenant is that Christ passes over the sins of His bride, the Church. His bride is free from shame, not because she is perfect, but because she has no fear that her lover will condemn her because of her sins or flaws. That is why justification by grace through faith is at the very heart of what makes a marriage work the way God designed it. Justification creates peace for us with God, and when experienced with each other, it creates the peaceful, shame-free, sacred, all-trusting security that God designed marriage to be, between an imperfect man and an imperfect woman, so that they have nothing more to hide and can be open with each other in every sense, where it can be said again, "they were both naked and were not ashamed."

There are two types of nakedness: physical nakedness and nakedness of the heart. If, as a man or a woman, you still need to put off the lights in the room to undress so that your spouse does not see your nakedness, you need to be mentally and spiritually regenerated. But that is not what we are talking about. We are talking about the nakedness of the heart – transparency, openness, sincerity, and truthfulness. The Bible teaches us to have a transparent relationship with our spouses, but our society and culture have taught us to keep some things away from each other. Our culture teaches us to keep the whole truth about what we earn away from our spouses so that they don't make unnecessary demands. But this has caused major problems in most homes because a situation where the woman thinks her husband earns more than what she already imagines, she would begin to make some demands and run the home based on what she thinks they need, not knowing whether they can actually afford it because nobody is telling her their true monthly financial status. However, if her husband comes open to say this is what I earn, she would be able to plan the family life around that means, save, or even encourage her husband to invest some.

Sarah called Abraham Lord. Lord is someone you submit to in everything. Openness is very important. Be open to each other. Some women would buy shares and build houses, and the husband will not know. Some men will have bank accounts, and the wife will not know. When you die, that money will become the bank's money; the money they did not work for. Some bankers are very dubious and wicked, so once they notice a dormant account that has been there for five years, they would investigate it to know the status of the owner, and when they discover that the person is dead, they will forge his credentials and empty that account. Openness is important. Let your spouse know everything about you. Tell your spouse about your past. When you go out and you probably sin, confess your sins to your spouse. **James 5** admonishes us to be transparent.

Confess to each other and pray for each other so that your relationship can be healed and made whole. If you keep your sins a secret, one day it will be blown to the open, and it will cause a bigger problem. The hymn, *'God Give Us Christian Home'* is one hymn that every family should meditatively sing every now and then.

Chapter Six
The Principle Of Love

In today's culture, we find that many use the word "love" so casually and flippantly. I often hear people say they want to get married because they are "in love." The truth is that many of these people are not so much "in love" as they are "in lust." No thanks to the mentality that worships fantasy in the pursuit of a love that "feels good;" this represents a selfish, sensual and sexual love, driven by raging hormones, and it's quite ecstatic. We dive in because it feels good, and when it ceases to feel good, we miss the feeling and begin to seek it elsewhere because this love is hormonally based, and the hormones that produce these ecstatic feelings cannot be sustained; they eventually slow down and wear off. Make no mistake about it; it takes much more than this ecstatic chemistry or feelings to keep a couple together for a lifetime. Little wonder many marriages fail while it's just getting started. The sooner we understand that love is not a feeling, the better for all involved. In this chapter, we shall be looking at the Principle of Love, and this begs the question:

WHAT IS LOVE?

Agape is the word that describes God's love for us, which means "loving you without conditions." It also explains how God wants us to love one another: sacrificial, unselfish, unconditional, and without expectations of something in return. This simply teaches us that love is a choice, and a commitment to give it all in good and bad times. Love is something that you keep choosing to do when you feel like it and when you don't feel like it; always seeking the good of the loved one. It is hard work, but one that is worth the effort. I love the way Christian Relationship and Family Counselor, Gary Smalley, puts it: *"Love is honour put into action regardless of the cost."* Simply put and ultimately, God is Love; this is the best definition of love, for love gives His life for even the one who is undeserving of love.

1 John 4:7-8 says,
"Beloved, let us love one another, for love is of God, and everyone who love is born of God and knows God.
He who does not love does not know God, for God is Love." (NKJV)

Firstly, you cannot be a vessel of love to another until you first fully belong to God because genuine lasting love is made possible through God; without the power of the Holy Spirit, we are incapable of making such unconditional commitment to another human being whose weaknesses are enough to push you to the edge. Thus, whoever must love for a lifetime must work with God. Jesus demonstrated Perfect love on the cross as He sacrificed His life for the world, for His Church. God is not expecting anything less between the husband and the wife. Most people marry because of love, which is mostly lust, in many cases. The love that God expects in marriage is beyond lust. Love is both vertical and horizontal, and that was demonstrated on the cross. He did that by spreading His hands wide on the cross reconciling us back to God. Therefore, for us to be able to give love to another person, be it a spouse, neighbour, friend, or a stranger, we must first love horizontally – love God. You cannot love another person if you cannot love God. If you love God, you will obey His commandment. As a man, you would love her, and as a woman, you would submit.

My wife and I were course mates back at the university. In fact, I submitted her final year project for her before going to submit mine. We graduated and left the university on the same day. I got a job two months after while she got a job much later. At a point, my salary was much more than hers. Then over time, her salary doubled mine with a new job. Today, with the position and the kind of job she does her salary overwhelms mine. But it takes a woman who loves God, understands the import of obeying God, and who knows the demands and expectations of God, to submit to her husband in such a situation.

We were both unbelievers when we got married. Back then, she used to call me Leky, a short expression of my name, but when we got married, she found a more suitable name that expresses her submission. If, as a man, you begin to sound it loud to your wife to submit to you, demanding submission aggressively, reminding her that you are the head of the home, then you have lost your place as the head of your home. You don't need to remind her; it is your love for her that will compel her to submit to you.

God did not tell the woman to love because love comes naturally to her. Submission does not. Likewise, the man, love does not come naturally to him. So, it takes a woman who loves and obeys God to submit to her husband. Most women are expressive lovers. The men, on the other hand, would usually not want to show it when they love a woman.

I remember when my wife and I were courting back then in university, she would do everything to hold me wherever we went no matter how hard I tried to resist her. Not because I did not love her, but because it was not natural for me; I was not wired that way. That is why God commands the husband to love because God knows us. Most women can tell you "I love you" a million times and never get tired of saying it, but it is tough for ninety-nine percent of men to say that to their spouse. It does not come naturally to them. When your marriage is tied to God it is easier for you to obey Him.

1 Cor. 13: 1-13 says,

"Though I speak with the tongues of men and of angels, but have not love, I have become sounding brass or a clanging cymbal.

And though I have the gift of prophecy, and understand all mysteries and all knowledge, and though I have all faith, so that I could remove mountains, but have not love, I am nothing.

And though I bestow all my goods to feed the poor, and though I give my body to be burned, but have not love, it profits me nothing.

Love suffers long and is kind; love does

not envy; love does not parade itself, is not puffed up; does not behave rudely, does not seek its own, is not provoked, thinks no evil; does not rejoice in iniquity, but rejoices in the truth; bears all things, believes all things, hopes all things, endures all things. Love never fails. But whether there are prophecies, they will fail; whether there are tongues, they will cease; whether there is knowledge, it will vanish away.

For we know in part and we prophesy in part. But when that which is perfect has come, then that which is in part will be done away.

When I was a child, I spoke as a child, I understood as a child, I thought as a child; but when I became a man, I put away childish things. For now we see in a mirror, dimly, but then face to face. Now I know in part, but then I shall know just as I also am known.

And now abide faith, hope, love, these three; but the greatest of these is love."

Love is not mere words. Love is action. Love does not punish. It does not threaten with divorce. Love does not envy, and it's not greedy. Where is it stated that I must earn more than my wife? Love does not envy the progress of the other. When a man is envious of his wife, the home will not stand because he will withhold any opportunity for her progress. When you withhold your support for your wife because of envy, you are hurting yourself. That is contrary to love.

Meanwhile, more often than not, in the heart of the woman whatever she has is for both of you and the good of your home. An envious heart withholds good things from others. I once met a woman who said that if her husband were to be rich, he would take a second wife. So, she made sure to destroy every opportunity for that man to make any meaningful progress. She went as far as using diabolic means to pull him down. I had to call the man and asked her to pray for him to break that evil spell.

Love forgives. There would be offences due to the differences in your backgrounds and ideologies. Both of you will surely have misunderstandings sometimes. Maybe God brought you together so you can also help correct those character flaws in the life of your partner.

Love is not self-centred. It is not "you" first but the other. There must be sacrifices. Most women are likely to leave the last piece of meat in the pot for the husband, but he should be able to sacrifice it for her or share it with her. With love, there's nothing like holding your ground that it must happen in a particular way. Love does not insist on having his way at all cost. Love is not self-centred; Jesus was not self-centred. He left His glory to save us because He could not allow the best of His creation to perish.

Love believes all things; you must trust your spouse. I'll tell you a story I heard about a particular couple. One eventful day while the husband was away at work, a big rat invaded their home. So, the woman cried out to her neighbours, and two young men went to help her to get rid of the rat. It was quite tasking for them, so they had to take off their shirts and remained in shorts while they ran around the house sweating. The woman joined in the chase, with just a piece of clothing wrapped around her chest, also sweating profusely. In the course of the event, her husband came into the house, saw all three sweating and jumped to the wrong conclusion. He carried his weapon to kill her because he judged her unfaithful. If not for neighbours who held him he could have committed murder. His action would have been unnecessary if he had any trust in her. His faith in her would have made him patient enough to listen and believe her story. If he had killed her or anyone that day, he would have ended up in prison simply because he lacked trust for his wife. I always say, do not believe anything about your spouse, even if you see him or her with someone else on the bed; until you see them in action, don't think it because it may just be a set-up. Put up with anything. Trust God always and do not look back.

> We must love as Christ loves:
> He loves unconditionally. **Rom. 5:5-10**
> He loves the Church sacrificially. **John 3:16**
> He loves redemptively. **Heb. 7:25**
> He loves us upfront. **Eph. 1:3-4**

He loves us completely. **Col. 2:1**0
He loves us consistently. **Heb. 13:8**
He loves us eternally. **Heb. 7:25**
He loves us immeasurably. **Eph. 3:20**

Even when we don't deserve it, Jesus still loves us.

FORGIVENESS

There's no way you can avoid offences in marriage because we are different in so many ways. Jesus admonishes us to forgive any offender for four hundred and ninety times per day. Meaning you should forgive all the way. I know a pastor who caught his wife in adultery. He wanted to divorce her, but when he realized that the Word of God kicked against it, he told her to go and live with his parents till his anger faded. Some people would say that Jesus permitted divorce on the basis of adultery, but the truth is that there's no reason for divorce. What is it that you have not done to offend Christ? Does it mean that since you became a Christian you have not sinned? When we live together, we offend each other because we have a relationship and are always together. But if we do not have a relationship, we won't pick offences with each other because we do not take note of each other's actions. If while walking on the road a stranger walk up to you and slaps you, won't you think he is a mad person and flee for your life? If you fight him, you too would be regarded as a mad man. That is because you do not have a relationship with the stranger. So, offences surely abound in marriage because you are always together; hence, you must also learn to forgive one another. Let's take a look at **Matt. 18:15-17**

Let's start with **Matt. 18:15:**

> *"Moreover, if your brother sins against you, go and tell him his fault between you and him alone. If he hears you, you have gained your brother."* (NKJV)

This scripture shows us how we should handle offences. It admonishes us on how to entreat those who offend us. It says the offended should approach the offender for peace and settlement. We, on the other hand, do the opposite; we wait for the offender to come to us first for peace, and in some cases, we even stay angry waiting for the offender to apologise, no matter how long it takes. That is not the biblical standard. That Scripture admonishes us to call the offender and tell them what they have done wrong and make peace. But most times, when the man of the house has offended his wife, he would still be expecting and waiting for her to come and apologise to him. Completely unbiblical!

The passage admonishes us to settle quarrels without involving other family members or friends, not even her family or yours. It is equally wrong to threaten your spouse that you will report him or her to his or her parents even if you are close to them. Tell your spouse what he or she has done wrong; she may not even be aware she offended you.

Matt. 18:16-17 goes on to say,

> *"But if he will not hear, take with you one or two more, that by the mouth of two or three witnesses every word may be established.*

> *And if he refuses to hear them, tell it to the church. But if he refuses even to hear the church, let him be to you like a heathen and a tax collector."* (NKJV)

Now, the Bible says call two or three people as witnesses if she would not listen. However, don't go calling two or three people that you know would be biased. I always advise people to take tough situations like this to God, especially when the other party refuses to own their faults. Prayerfully commit the heart of that person to God. And if your spouse still stands on their wrong grounds, look for an elder who has a Christian testimony in his or her family.

There's this story of a pastor who counselled a particular couple whenever they had problems. He was very good at giving wise counsel. He never did it alone; his wife must always be by his side. So, the couple trusted his counsels and respected them for it. It happened that one Sunday morning that this young couple had a terrible fight at home, and in the fit of anger, they both sped off to report each other to the pastor. As they approached his house, they began to hear a noise, and they pressed on. Lo and behold, as they came closer, they saw the pastor beating his wife. Immediately, they turned, went back home and advised each other on the right things to do as a couple. They gave themselves counsel.

So, when you want to take your case to anybody, you must be sure they have lived and are still living the Word of God. I was speaking to one of my bosses some time ago, who had assaulted his wife. I questioned his action and he said it was necessary to beat one's wife sometimes. I was not even born again then, but when I told him that I had never lifted my finger against my wife, he did not believe it.

Some men believe in beating their spouse, so if you carry your case to such a person, he would advise you to beat your wife at the slightest provocation as a corrective measure. Don't take your case to such people but to those who have a good home and would take up your matter to God as a prayer project. Don't go for counselling with a mind to divorce but a mind of reconciliation. The other person does not have to change immediately, but you must forgive. Go, believing God for a change after the counselling session because you cannot change anybody. You may get hurt trying to change the other person by force. Only God can change a person. Hence, **Col. 3:12-15** admonishes,

> *"Therefore, as the elect of God, holy and beloved, put on tender mercies, kindness, humility, meekness, longsuffering; bearing with one another, and forgiving one another, if anyone has a complaint against another; even as Christ forgave you, so you also must do. But above all these things put on love, which is the bond of perfection. And let the peace of God rule in your hearts, to which also you were called in one body; and be thankful."* (NKJV)

COMMUNICATION

The biggest problem in many marriages is a communication barrier. Everyone may not be able to express themselves as their partners do, but each of us needs to learn how to communicate with our spouses. Women talk naturally and easily; they love to talk to feel better, to process things, to open up for intimacy, and to deliver on her help ministry. The woman does not only love to talk; she "needs" to talk because she is relational and auditory in the way she processes information in order to effectively serve her purpose. However, talking does not come naturally and easily to a man, as he is more visual than auditory; while a man silently pleads, *"spare me the details, get to the point please"*, the woman loves details, and so, most men often try to interrupt the process by jumping in to cut it short with some brief response or advice, and sometimes even a grunt. This only creates friction that eventually spills over negatively into the home. It is vital to understand that for your wife to help you effectively, you both must have to communicate more sufficiently. Communication is a soothing medicine for the soul, and thus, a necessary ingredient for success in any marriage. Let's look at two Scriptures that buttress communication:

Proverbs 25:11

"A word fitly spoken is like apples of gold in settings of silver." (NKJV)

The two parties must communicate. They must talk to each other in companionship. Sometimes when good intentions are not properly put together, it may cause or create a problem. Maybe a lack of sufficient communication between Adam and Eve must have pushed Eve to go hanging out with the talkative snake to gossip about what God said and what He did not say, which eventually lead to their fall. Many marriages have failed for lack of sufficient communication, and I use the word "sufficient" with emphasis because some communications are no communications at all. For instance, your wife asks you, *"what did your boss say about the leave you requested so we can travel together?"* And you respond, *"not much."* You have not communicated at all! Because your response could mean either of two things: it's okay or it's not okay to take the leave. Now, imagine a situation where she then works with the assumption that it is okay for you to travel believing that "you know" you both need the time off together, and goes ahead to plan the vacation, only for you to turn around and tell her you did not tell her it was okay. Yes, you did not tell her it was okay, but you did not tell her it was not okay either. Your wife asked you that question because she really wanted to know the details and plan with the details you give her, not to be left confused or empty-handed to figure it out; she is not a mind reader. Isn't it amazing how something so simple can mess up a beautiful moment in a relationship? An unambiguous response would have gone a long way to squash all argument and aggravation, and benefit both of you.

Sufficient communication between a couple is absolutely vital; the lack of it can be detrimental to the health of the marriage. When I think about communication in marriage, the fall of Adam and Eve keeps playing on my mind, and I can't help but say it is safe to imagine that when Eve must have asked Adam about the forbidden tree in the garden that Adam, in the typical men manner, may have simply said to Eve, *"just leave that tree, don't touch it, except you want to die."* This is insufficient communication; he has simply not given her the proper instruction that God gave him, which God expected Adam to share with his 'help meet' to keep her fully informed, and thus, make her an effective helper. Why did I say this? Now, pay attention; after the serpent asked Eve, if God really said you must not eat from any tree in the garden. Notice what Eve said to the serpent in **Gen. 3:2-3** (NIV), *"The woman said to the serpent, we may eat fruit from the trees in the garden, but God did say, 'you must not eat fruit from the tree that is in the middle of the garden, and **you must not touch it**, or you will die."*

Wrong answer! God never told Adam that they could not **"touch"** the tree, God said, *"you must **not eat** from the tree of the knowledge of good and evil, for when you eat from it you will certainly die"*- **Gen. 2:17**. He said don't **"eat!"** God couldn't have said don't touch. How will they tend the tree if they were not to touch it? The serpent noticed and capitalised on Eve's ignorance! Careless, insufficient explanation keeps people working in ignorance and makes it easy for them to fail.

It is safe to say that Adam's insufficient communication made it much easier for the crafty serpent to deceive Eve, especially when she saw that the serpent climbed and touched the tree as it spoke to her, and it did not die, and then she must have touched it too and nothing happened. That was convincing enough, so naturally, the next step will be let's try the "eating" part and see what happens; so, she did. Too late to turn back now! As couples we must endeavor to communicate at deeper levels with one another. A great marriage takes hard work, but it is work that is worth it in the long run, so let's put in the effort on communicating better.

Let's see the second Scripture, **Proverbs 15:1**

> *"A soft answer turns away wrath, But a harsh word stirs up anger."* (NKJV)

Communication gets worse when we speak harsh words to each other. Some people's tongues are as sharp as a blade. Most women talk a lot. Someone once told me that the reason why women talk is that they cannot fight. It's not bad to talk but let your word be seasoned with salt. Let each party treat the other with the utmost respect in their speech. Make polite requests and not "demand" forcefully. As a woman, you can even send your husband on errands if you make your requests politely. Learn to use the word, please and learn to say thank you. Don't wait to point out errors in the things each of you do or do not do. Appreciate each other's efforts, no matter how little. If the food she cooks today is salty, you need not scold her for it; thank her for the good food. Thank him for the times he goes out or travels and remembers to buy you gifts.

Appreciate each other in the times when you both enjoyed sex; talk about it, in so doing you learn more of what each enjoys and make it even better. This is one thing that destroys the home; there is nothing wrong with talking about the experience with your spouse. It's funny how a man finds it easier to share with friends about his sexual escapades with a prostitute than to talk to his wife about his experience in bed. You both need to discuss your sexual issues with each other. A couple came to me for counselling. They were at my place till 2am going back and forth. The man eventually had to speak up that the wife deprives him of sex. When I asked her why. She said she didn't like sex. I told her that she just has to "love" it. That has been the problem for two years. However, the man also has a major part to play in helping her love it by finding out what will make it enjoyable for her; this is made possible if they share their experiences and sexual needs with each other; tell him or her how you like to be touched. Do not be shy about it; the Bible says, *"they were both naked and were not ashamed."* It's your right as a married couple, nothing to be ashamed of with each other.

Furthermore, you must both learn to say sorry, especially for men, learn to apologise. If you don't say sorry when you need to, you may destroy your home. I apologise to my wife when I offend her deeply so that my prayers will not be hindered. You know you are wrong, yet you can't say sorry; you can't say sorry to a woman you have offended, and you think the car or cloth gift would speak better. Do you think she has forgotten? The pain is still right there. The only thing she needs is just a hug, and a simple "I am sorry". You'll discover later that she may not even use any of those gifts as long as that pain is still in her heart; yes, she may have received it but may never use them until she is healed within because you have offended her. And if you always fail to apologise, it will keep building up until the day that she will explode or even the score. When that happens, it will be like a perforated balloon, and your relationship may never be the same anymore.

Avoid shouting when communicating with each other. Any information passed in anger may not be received well, and it may be given an interpretation that was not intended.

Control your temper, always remind yourself of the outcome and unpleasantness your anger or reaction can cause at home. Even children resist being shouted on. Remember, the purpose of communication is to make your partner understand the point or information you are trying to pass across.

Learn to say words that are edifying and

gratifying instead of words that put each other down.

Celebrate your success together and encourage yourselves in time of failure. Realise that you are not competing but are meant to complement each other.

Unless you talk with each other, it is almost impossible for anyone to know what is going on in the other person's mind. So, do not try to read the mind of your spouse, speak out, and don't expect him or her to know what you are thinking; this only leads to conflicts, misunderstandings, and unnecessary friction in the home.

PRAYER

A family that prays together stays together. Prayer will bring everything together. Remember when the scriptures talk about the whole amour of God in **Eph. 6**, after mentioning all the amours; in **verse 18** it says we should pray with all manner of prayers. Prayer is submission to God. Give God your home. Prayer must be done together. Schedule a private vigil in your room with your wife. Encourage family devotions as frequently as possible, even where you have a very tight work schedule. The secret of a successful family is God. Why some children succeed more than others is family prayers, not only mere intelligence. This song that I love to sing couldn't be more apt; it says:

> *Except thou build it, Father,*
> *The house is built in vain.*
> *Except thou Saviour bless it,*
> *The joy will turn to pain*
> *But nought can bring the marriage*
> *Of heart being made one.*
> *And love thy Spirit hallows,*
> *In endless love begun.*

Except the Lord builds a family, that house is built on sinking sand. Except God blesses the marriage, one small push and that marriage will wobble. There is nothing that can bring to nought the marriage of two hearts that have been bound together by God. In every marriage, there would be a time of storms and shakings; there would be a time of flood and wind, but when God is the binding force of that home, all the season will pass by, and the home will still stand.

Conclusively, we must understand that there is "order" in the house of God because God is a God of order, this is evident in all of His creation, and more so, order is an essential rule of success in all areas of life. Remember, it takes much more than ecstatic chemistry or feeling good between two people to keep them together for a lifetime. It takes aligning with God and "choosing" to love your spouse without conditions, in and out of all seasons; there are no exceptions.

Chapter Seven
God Hates Divorce

In the past few decades, the modern culture sledgehammer has attacked the marriage institution vehemently, and the evidence of the havoc it is wreaking is everywhere, as the number of married couples getting divorced continues to rise at an alarming rate. We have allowed the world's ideals that 'deify self' to seep into the fabric of the sanctity of marriage. The stigma against divorce is no more, and the lines are blurred between that which is sacred and that which is carnal, forgetting that *"God made them male and female, and for this reason, a man will leave his father and mother and be united to his wife, and the two will become one flesh"* Mark 10:6-8).

There is no longer a prejudice against divorce; instead it is now the reverse, a prejudice against any effort to make the marriage work, as many continue to harden their hearts, choosing to believe the world fallacy that a life spent with the same partner is both unrealistic and unworthy, especially if not happy in the marriage. No; the world has it all twisted and wrong. It was never meant to be like that.

In the beginning, we see God Himself set out to complete one of the central designs of creation, the union of a man and a woman in marriage. An institution He designed with the intent to model the covenant relationship between Christ and His Church. Thus, if the ultimate design of marriage is to represent the unbreakable covenant love between Christ and His Church, it then means that no human being has the right to break a marriage covenant. Little wonder Jesus did not settle for the divorce provision Moses made in **Deut. 24:1-4**:

> *"If a man marries a woman who becomes displeasing to him because he finds*

*something indecent about her, and he writes
her a certificate of divorce, gives it to her
and sends her from his house, and if after
she leaves his house she becomes the wife of
another man, and her second husband
dislikes her and writes her a certificate of
divorce, gives it to her and sends her from his
house, or if he dies, then her first husband,
who divorced her, is not allowed to marry her
again after she has been defiled. That would
be detestable in the eyes of the Lord. Do not
bring sin upon the land the Lord your God
is giving you as an inheritance."* (NIV)

It is important to note that Moses made this
provision for divorce as a result of the hardness
of the heart of the people, as we can see in
Matt. 19:7-8,

*"Why then," they asked, "did Moses
command that a man give his wife a
certificate of divorce and send her away? Jesus
replied, Moses permitted you to divorce
your wives because your hearts were hard.
But it was not this way from the
beginning."* (NIV)

The wickedness borne out of the hardened heart of man forced Moses to offer the people a way out of the marriage covenant, rather than let them continue to unleash violence against each other, but God never made provision for divorce in His design of marriage. Thus, Jesus was not going to let any human being, prophet or not, define the boundaries and proffer carnal solutions to a sacred institution. Jesus knew the mind of the Father concerning marriage, and He came to the world to reveal and do only His Father's will; therefore, He opens the eyes of His disciples and teaches the Pharisees the core truth about divorce, as He concludes in **Mark 10:9:**

"Therefore, what God has joined together, let not man separate." (NKJV).

Simply put, since God is the creator and definer of marriage, only God has the authority to break a marriage, and He does it only by death, not divorce, and that is why the biblical marriage vows have only one limitation: *"Till death do us part,"* or *"As long as we both shall live."* And even that limitation of death in marriage has its own boundaries: Death can only be by God; nobody has the right to take his or her own life or take another person's life.

Today, we live in times where divorce has become so rampant in the society that it's no longer news if a marriage celebrated with pomp and pageantry collapses just a few months after the wedding. The rate of divorce nowadays has become more alarming than we have ever known in time past. Statistically, a large percentage of marriages are going through emotional problems, and if care is not taken, it may end in separation or total breakdown that results in divorce. Now, that is the point God never wants any of His creation to degenerate to; His stance on divorce is made clear in **Mal. 2:16**

> *"For the Lord God of Israel says that He hates divorce, for it covers one's garment with violence," Says the Lord of hosts. "Therefore take heed to your spirit that you do not deal treacherously."* (NKJV)

If God says He hates divorce that settles it.

Divorce is detrimental to God's purpose for marriage. It is disobedience to God, and it works against His plan for the family. There is no excuse good enough for husband and wife to divorce. In any relationship, there will sometimes be misunderstanding, quarrel, and even conflicts but our ability to be humble enough, communicate rightly and show maturity and respect for each other's opinion will determine the way our relationship will go.

Everything that will succeed in life requires hard work and marriage is not an exception. In fact, a stable and peaceful home requires more hard work than any other endeavour, as temptations abound to test the solidity of the union; this is so because the devil is interested in our homes. The first visitor Adam and Eve received after marriage, other than God, was the tempter, the devil - **Gen.3: 1**,

"Now the serpent was more cunning than any beast of the field which the Lord God had made. And he said to the woman,

"Has God indeed said, 'You shall not eat of every tree of the garden'?" (NKJV)

The devil knew that God had a plan for mankind; I imagine that he was even envious of the position and honour bestowed on man by God and he intended to bring man down, which he succeeded in doing. Thank God for the redemptive work of our Lord Jesus on the cross, man was reconciled back to God. The devil has not stopped that battle, and so we must be vigilant as he can use any means to pull down any family that is not conscious of his devices.

For God, marriage is a point of no return; once you have entered, you are expected to stay in it for life. It is the only institution you enter, and you receive a certificate at the beginning of the journey; receiving the certificate in advance indicates that you must do everything to succeed in it. No excuse for failure. But more importantly, God outlawed divorce in the Bible. Let us consider the following scriptures:

According to **Matt. 5:31-32**, the only ground

for divorce is on account of fornication. Now, what is fornication? It is premarital sex. Which means the party concerned are not yet married; thus, at this point, separation is allowed. This point is further emphasized in **Matt. 19:3-10**

"The Pharisees also came to Him, testing Him, and saying to Him, "Is it lawful for a man to divorce his wife for just any reason?" And He answered and said to them, "Have you not read that He who made them at the beginning 'made them male and female,' and said, 'For this reason a man shall leave his father and mother and be joined to his wife, and the two shall become one flesh'? So then, they are no longer two but one flesh. Therefore, what God has joined together, let not man separate." They said to Him, "Why then did Moses command to give a certificate of divorce, and to put her away?" He said to them, "Moses, because of the hardness of your hearts, permitted you to divorce your wives, but from the beginning it was not so. And I say to you, whoever divorces his wife, except for sexual immorality, and marries another, commits

adultery; and whoever marries her who is divorced commits adultery." His disciples said to Him, "If such is the case of the man with his wife, it is better not to marry." (NKJV).

In the Jewish culture, once a woman is betrothed to a man, she can be referred to as his wife, as she becomes off-limits to other men, but the two of them must not come together as husband and wife until they are legally married. Let's see the account of Joseph with the Angel of the Lord in **Matt 1: 18-25**:

"Now the birth of Jesus Christ was as follows: After His mother, Mary was betrothed to Joseph, before they came together, she was found with child of the Holy Spirit. Then Joseph, her husband, being a just man, and not wanting to make her a public example, was minded to put her away secretly. But while he thought about these things, behold, an angel of the Lord appeared to him in a dream, saying, "Joseph, son of David, do not be afraid to take to you Mary your wife, for that which is conceived in her is of the Holy Spirit. And she will

bring forth a Son, and you shall call His name JESUS, for He will save His people from their sins." So all this was done that it might be fulfilled which was spoken by the Lord through the prophet, saying: "Behold, the virgin shall be with child, and bear a Son, and they shall call His name Immanuel," which is translated, "God with us." Then Joseph, being aroused from sleep, did as the angel of the Lord commanded him and took to him his wife, and did not know her till she had brought forth her firstborn Son. And he called His name JESUS."

Note in the account above that Mary was espoused to Joseph but not yet married. This could be likened to engagement or family introduction in our setting. However, they were referred to as husband and wife. Thus, divorce on the ground of fornication refers to a separation between two people who were engaged but not yet joined together legally in marriage before one of them commits fornication. Do not be deceived; God does not approve divorce after marriage. Jesus knew this truth and made it clear to the Pharisees that it was because of the hardness of the heart of the people that Moses, not God, permitted divorce, noting that *"but it was not so from the beginning"*

Just like every good thing God created from the beginning, the devil works relentlessly to destroy and pervert the original plan of God for marriage, and any man or woman that is not sensitive enough will allow the devil to have his way. The Bible says, *"give no room to the devil."* Thus, many reasons account for breakdown of peace and harmony in the homes that could eventually lead to divorce, among them are these major ones:

1. **A misunderstanding of the position or role of money in the home:** What God has joined together; money should not put asunder. If the man or woman sees money as the ultimate, it may lead to competition, inordinate ambition, pride, and other things that can cause disharmony in the home.

Money is good; lack of money in the home can cause conflict, but when there is love and money is placed in its rightful position in the home, the couple can still live happily and fulfilled with little money.

A heart that is not submitted to God will find it difficult to submit his pocket to God or anybody. It will be easier for the couple to jointly determine how to spend their money if the two are accountable to God. A man and a woman that can pledge their life and body to themselves should be able to submit their money to each other. Money should not be the master but a messenger in the home. When we have this understanding, our finance should not be a source of disharmony in the home.

2. **Lies and deceit in any relationship destroys it:** The couple must be sincere and honest with each other. They must be open to each other.

3. **Pride and a feeling of superiority can cause a breakdown in any relationship:** The Bible says in **Eph. 5:21**, *"submitting to one another in the fear of God."* Many husbands put so much emphasis on **Vs.22**, which says, *"wives submit"*, leaving out the verse preceding it that demands mutual respect from each other. **Phil. 2:3-4** *"Let nothing be done through selfish*

ambition or conceit, but in lowliness of mind, let each esteem others better than himself." Let each of you look out not only for his or her own interests but also for the interests of your spouse.

4. **Infidelity:** This is extramarital affairs or unfaithfulness to one's spouse. When a partner cheats on the other partner, it causes disharmony and brings hurt, which may destroy the marriage. The Bible speaks explicitly against the defilement of the marriage bed. *"Marriage is honorable among all, and the bed undefiled; but fornicators and adulterers God will judge."* **Heb. 13:4** (NKJV)

5. **Interference of third-party:** You are both responsible for the success of your marriage. Third-party should not be allowed to meddle in the affairs of the couple. Settle your differences yourself. Every family have their challenges that they are trying to cope with. Nobody will stand for you before God if you have to give an account of your marriage to God. The man is expected to present his wife to God just as Christ will present the Church to God without spot, wrinkle and

irreproachable. You cannot pass the buck to your friend or relatives. **Eph. 5:26-27**.

6. **Unnecessary competition:** You are not competing with each other; you are meant to be complementing each other. Nobody is perfect and that is why God brought you together to complete each other. Competition breeds rivalry, and this eventually results in the breakdown of peace in the home.

However, while God hates divorce or putting away, if the continuous habitation of the couple becomes life-threatening and finding an immediate solution to their problems becomes impossible, the couple may be advised to separate for a while. A couple that decides to separate should know that none of them can marry any other until the death of the partner. **I Cor. 7:10-11**:

> *"Now to the married I command, yet not I but the Lord: A wife is not to depart from her husband. But even if she does depart, let her remain unmarried or be reconciled to her husband. And a husband is not to divorce his wife."* (NKJV)

In conclusion, marriage is a lifetime commitment, and designed to demonstrate the love relationship between the Lord Jesus Christ and the Church that He loves so much and paid for her with His blood. Holding on to this profound truth, brethren, remember that when the centre can no longer hold, things fall apart. There is no centre that holds as firmly and as forever as God, so make Him the centre of your life and your marriage to hold you together, never to fall apart. Also, endeavour to keep the flame of love in your marriage burning; do not let it be quenched for any reason.

For those yet to marry, it is wise to seek God's face for your partner, don't just pick anyone from anywhere or nowhere to marry; it is detrimental to you and to your purpose in life. *"If any man marries wrongly, even the devil will leave you alone because he knows you are finished already."* (Fb).